Racialized Identities

Racialized Identities

Race and Achievement among African American Youth

Na'ilah Suad Nasir

Stanford University Press
Stanford, California

Stanford University Press
Stanford, California

Printed in the United States of America on acid-free, archival-quality paper

Library of Congress Cataloging-in-Publication Data

Nasir, Na'ilah Suad, author.
  Racialized identities : race and achievement among African American youth /
Na'ilah Suad Nasir.
    pages cm
  Includes bibliographical references and index.
  ISBN 978-0-8047-6018-8 (cloth : alk. paper) — ISBN 978-0-8047-6019-5 (pbk. :
alk. paper)
  1. African American youth—Education. 2. African Americans—Race identity.
3. African American students—Social conditions. 4. Academic achievement—
United States. I. Title.
  LC2717.N37 2012
  371.829'96073—dc22
                            2011007294

Typeset by Bruce Lundquist in 11/13.5 Adobe Garamond Pro

This book is dedicated to my family:
Baayan, Leya, Asé, Sajdah, and Ajeyei.
You are my strength and my light.

Contents

Acknowledgments

I am deeply indebted to an intricate network of people for my presence in the world and in the academy. First, of course, my parents, who made sure that education was first in my life. Special thanks to my mother, Leslie Stone, who has been a constant source of support with my children and who has transcribed countless interviews over the years.

In addition to my biological parents, I also have several academic parents, who nurtured my scholarship and were true advocates, even when I didn't know it. During my graduate school years at UCLA, there were many: Geoffrey Saxe, who is now my colleague at UC Berkeley, has been a quiet and constant source of support and gentle, well-targeted feedback. I channel my "inner Geoff" often in my advising roles with students. Mike Rose, who made the academy seem possible simply by being such a fabulous scholar and down-to-earth human being, and by engaging my ideas, half-baked as they were. Kris Gutierrez, who has been a staunch mentor and friend, who showed me that one could be a fly diva *and* be brilliant, and that mentorship could be personal and professional. In my years on the faculty at Stanford, Jim Greeno and Dan Schwartz read early drafts of some of the work presented in this book and told me what my point was when I wasn't quite sure. Linda Darling-Hammond and Arnetha Ball made me feel at home on "the farm" and taught me much about teaching and navigating university spaces. Bill Damon provided a great example of public scholarship and was a valued colleague. From Ray McDermott, I learned that the academy could be a playground for ideas and that students' dissertation hearings could be sport.

My dean at Stanford, Deborah Stipek, was a pleasure to work under and always let me know that she believed in my work. My new academic home at Berkeley has also been the source of tremendous support. Janelle Scott, Lisa Garcia-Bedolla, Erin Murphy-Graham, Patricia Baquedano-Lopez, Tina Trujillo, and Laura Sterponi have made me feel blessed to be a part of a cohort of women scholars who are also fabulous mothers and dedicated friends. I look forward to many years of friendship and colleagueship ahead. Dan Perlstein has provided lots of fodder for thought by challenging my work and resisting all forms of conformity. Frank Worrell has been a mentor and example of responsible academic leadership. And finally, Dean David Pearson made the impossible happen in Berkeley in one fell swoop and has been amazingly supportive of my work. Thanks for bringing me to Berkeley! In addition to the personal and professional lessons, I have benefited from the important scholarship of all the folks mentioned above.

I have also had the great pleasure to be a part of several research collectives, which have each influenced my thinking and broadened my horizons. The CHiLD (Collaborative for Human Learning and Diversity) research collective was a life-changing experience for me, and working with such a talented group of scholars was some of the greatest fun I've had in the academy; thanks to Carol Lee, Barbara Rogoff, Kris Gutierrez, Margaret Beale Spencer, Ann Rosebery, Beth Warren, Fred Erikson, Jelani Mandara, Bart Hirsch, Marjorie Orelleana, Norma Gonzalez, and the many others who made those meetings so rich. The LIFE (Learning in Formal and Informal Environments) Center has been an ongoing source of intellectual stimulation and colleagueship; thanks to John Bransford, Roy Pea, Dan Schwartz, Nora Sabelli, Phil Bell, Reed Stevens, Brigid Barron, Andy Meltzoff, Pat Kuhl, and Bill Penuel. The Comparative Center for the Study of Race and Ethnicity at Stanford was a haven on campus and provided an interdisciplinary perspective on issues of race, culture, and ethnicity; thanks to Claude and Dorothy Steele, Hazel Marcus, Anthony Antonio, Jennifer Eberhardt, George Frederickson, Al Camarillo, and many others. The Berkeley Diversity Research Initiative and the African American Studies Department has helped me find a home on the Berkeley campus and has supported my forays into important new territory on race; thanks to Gibor Basri, Charles Henry, and Chris Edley.

I offer a special thanks to two women whom I admire tremendously, both for their intellectual contributions to my thinking and for their modeling of how one can be a serious scholar and a dedicated wife and mother, and still find time to be an activist. Carol Lee and Margaret Beale Spencer have been to me what I hope to be for the scholars coming after me—a source of wisdom, kindness, and strength. I draw both from the depth, rigor, and integrity of your scholarship, and from the light of your example. I thank you ladies from the bottom of my heart.

Many thanks to the various collaborators on the research presented in this book: Jamal Cooks, Amina Jones, Milbrey McLaughlin, Michael Davis, Kathleen O'Conner, and Grace Atukpawu. The thinking in these pages is also yours.

I have been blessed to have some of the best students one could dream of: thanks to Vicki Hand, Ben Kirshner, Aisha Toney, Michael Davis, Grace Atukpawu, and those still in the pipeline, Amina Jones, Kathleen O'Connor, Sarah Wischnia, Jessica Tsang, Shayna Sullivan, Nicole Louie, Niral Shah, and Kihana Ross.

Special thanks to Erin Murphy-Graham and the anonymous reviewers for reading drafts of these chapters and offering such valuable feedback. Tryphenia Peele-Eady—one my oldest colleagues in the academy—also offered invaluable feedback on the draft manuscript. Many thanks to you. Thanks to Kate Wahl at Stanford University Press for your patience and responsiveness.

My personal network of family and friends has been a source of strength and laughter. To my sisters (biological and acquired)—Denisha Dawson, Estrella Jones, Tryphenia Peele-Eady, Gina Yarbrough, Adilah Bilal, Jasiyah Ngeno, Yolanda Majors, and Maria Trejo—you all are my daily inspiration and I find great truth and humor in sharing our lives.

To my children—Leya, Asé, Sajdah, and Ajeyei—without you all I have no idea who I'd be, or what I'd do with all of my time. Leya, you have been my road dog from the beginning. It's amazing to see you move into adulthood. Asé, you are a ray of sunshine in my life and great fodder for my parental and personal growth. Sajdah, I am continually amazed by your focus and can't wait until you get to travel the world. Gotta get that passport! Ajeyei, it has been a joy to watch you discover the world. I enjoy each of you immensely—you give my life meaning.

And finally, to my husband, Baayan Bakari, the smartest man I know, who remembers to nurture me even when I forget; you are my heart, my love, and it is because of your strength that I have the courage to face the world every day.

Racialized Identities

Introduction

THIS BOOK is about identity processes and their relation to learning and schooling as they play out in the lives of African American youth.[1] It is a culmination of, and reflection on, years of research inside and outside of schools and draws on findings from several studies of African American adolescents. Some of these studies focused on the learning and identity that were afforded in out-of-school settings, such as basketball, dominoes, and track and field. Other studies explored the ways that identity processes took shape in schools—almost always urban schools, which struggled to establish an intellectual culture and build the infrastructure and practices to support students' academic potential.

My research on the identities of African American students takes place against a backdrop of widespread inequity in our schools nationally. Schools attended by African American students tend to be characterized by lower grading standards, less (and less deep) coverage of curriculum material, and less money spent per pupil and are more likely to be in physical disrepair (Darling-Hammond, 2000, 2010; Ferguson, 2007; Oakes, 2004; Orfield, 2001). Teachers in such schools are less likely to be credentialed, are newer to the profession, and are more likely to teach by "drill-and-kill" methods (Darling-Hammond, Williamson, and Hyler, 2008; Lankford, Loeb, and Wyckoff, 2002). To make matters worse, both communities and schools are increasingly segregated, perpetuating and intensifying the unequal distribution of resources and the concentration of poverty (Kozol, 2005; Massey, 2007; Orfield, 2001).

Not surprisingly, given the unequal playing field, African American students are more likely than their white and Asian American peers to drop out before graduating from high school (Balfanz and Letgers, 2004; National Center for Education Statistics, 2007), score lower on standardized tests (National Center for Education Statistics, 2005), take fewer advanced placement courses (Gamoran, 1992; Oakes, 2004), and are less likely to attend college (U.S. Census Bureau, 2008). Achievement differences by race begin as early as the fourth grade and persist all the way through college. By the twelfth grade, African American students are about four years behind white and Asian American students (Haycock, Jerald, and Huang, 2001). The national graduation rate for African American male students is around 47 percent, compared with 78 percent for white male students. (Schott Foundation, 2010). Clearly, race is an important consideration in understanding national achievement patterns among African American students.

However, I am ambivalent about reporting (yet again) these widespread patterns of educational inequity by race. On the one hand, I think it is important to acknowledge the full extent of the challenge that African American students face as they seek to be educated in public schools in the United States. On the other hand, I worry that these achievement patterns have become one of the primary ways we frame the conversation around academic achievement and schooling for African American students—leaving African American students and communities to be defined by relative lack and ignoring the myriad of strengths and tremendous resilience that exist in urban schools and African American communities (Gutierrez, 2008; Lee, 2008; Martin, 2009; Spencer, 2008).

In this book, therefore, I not only focus on the challenges that social and educational stratification pose for youths' identities and access to learning but also highlight the possibilities for positive learning and identity trajectories. I view learning and identity simultaneously as individual processes that involve agency and personal sense-making and as social processes deeply influenced by social context, norms, and interactions with others in learning settings.

Critical to my work has been attending to both the individual learning and identity processes in which young people are engaged and the social, cultural, and institutional spaces in which these processes take place. Students' constructions of themselves racially and academically are deeply and profoundly influenced by the multiple settings that students negotiate daily, including but not limited to school settings, neighborhood settings, and families. Students' identities are also influenced by the broader societal context that perpetuates racial inequities on multiple levels and constrains identity choices for African American youth. In particular, media portrayals and stereotypes of African American youth may have important implications for the identity choices African American youth perceive for themselves (Spencer, 2006).

It is a fascinating time in our nation's history to study race and identity for African Americans. As I write this, the United States of America has just sworn in its first African American president. Some have argued that this event marked or punctuated a transition to a "postracial" America, where race is no longer a determinant for experience or opportunity (Blackwell, Kwoh, and Pastor, 2002; Steele, 2008). And yet, days before the inauguration, an unarmed twenty-two-year-old African American man, Oscar Grant, was shot to death while handcuffed and lying on the ground by a transit police officer in Oakland, California (Bulwa, Buchanan, and Yi, 2009). No action was taken against the officer until people took to the streets in protest. Months later, he was found guilty of manslaughter. This contradiction between being the first largely white nation to elect an African American man as president and being a country where an African American man can still lose his life because of police brutality is striking. As Blackwell, Kwoh, and Pastor (2002) note, "While there have been economic and social gains among people of color in the latter part of the 20th century, inequity remains a facet of the American social order" (48). It is a time both of great promise and of the manifestation of age-old stereotypes about African Americans.

The election of Barack Obama also raised several relevant and interesting dilemmas about race. Some debated whether Obama was African American at all, given the fact that his mother was white. Others worried about the ways that his campaign approached the issue of race, or failed to approach it. Steele (2008) argued that Obama's sophisticated use of race and triggering of white racial guilt led to his election, but even very conservative Steele concluded that the racial inequities in our country are pressing and are unlikely to be resolved by the Obama presidency. The controversy over the use of race in the Obama campaign, and over Obama's personal racial identity (what makes him black or "not black enough"?), signals some of the important concerns with which this book wrestles.

In this book, I attempt to portray the complexity of identity as it occurs in both school and out-of-school settings, the ways that these settings make identities available to young African Americans, and the ways that students make choices about who they are and who they want to be. I consider learning identities, academic identities, and racialized identities, as well as the interactions among them. At times, the data make apparent the ways in which African American students are struggling to integrate these multiple identities. At other times, the data illustrate how students resolve the racialized/academic identity struggles that are so prominent in the media and in the scholarly literature, and how learning settings can be organized such that these struggles are not posed so extremely for students.

Race is a particularly challenging aspect of identity to study because it is lived and enacted subtly on multiple levels of experience. One challenge in studying race (particularly in relation to individuals) is the trouble that comes with assuming that members of racial groups are homogenous—in other words, essentializing. When we essentialize, we oversimplify the construct of race and fail to address the nuance and complexity that are inherent in the multiple ways we live race (Davidson, 1996; Lewis, 2003; Pollock, 2005; Skinner and Schafer, 2009). One resolution to this problem may be to understand that the racial boxes we use for the purposes of categorization are not deterministic; rather, they are rough ways of indexing the cultural practices and experiences of people in this highly racialized society. It is in this spirit that I use racial categories in this book. In other words, I assume both regularity within groups and variability (Gutiérrez, 2004; Lee, 2007).

Throughout this book, I use the term "racialized" identities, rather than "racial" identities. In my view, the term "racialized identities" signals my underlying assumption about the fluidity and social construction of racial boundaries. Keating (1995) draws on Omi and Winant (1994) and critical race theorists to argue that the continued use of racial categories to describe and define people perpetuates the assumption that race is a sociobiological concept and fails to problematize the racist roots of racial categorization. She issues a caution: "theorists who attempt to deconstruct 'race' often inadvertently reconstruct it by reinforcing the belief in permanent, separate racial categories. Although they emphasize the artificial, politically and economically motivated nature of all racial classifications, their continual analysis of racialized identities undercuts their belief that 'race' is a constantly changing sociohistorical concept, not a biological fact" (902). While I wholeheartedly agree that we must be careful about the ways that our work can reinforce existing racial hierarchies and boundaries, I also find that failing to discuss, describe, and account for issues of race in learning settings and educational processes renders us blind to the ways that racialization can play an important role in learning and schooling. Thus, my use of the term "racialized identities" is an effort to honor the idea that race (and thus racial identities) is not an inherent category but rather is *made racial* through social interaction, positioning, and discourse. These identities are continually reinforced and reinvented as researchers write about and study students.

Skinner and Schafer (2009) view this attention to racialized identities and the construction and maintenance of racial boundaries (which are part and parcel of how these identities are constructed in social settings) as key to our understanding of the experience of racial subjects in school settings. They argue, "We must pay close attention to the ways in which racial identities (or identifications), knowledge, and power are produced within educational institutions structured by ever-changing forms of racial oppression" (277). Thus, a focus on racialized identities in school settings is an important aspect of understanding how power and privilege are reproduced in such settings. However, we must be careful about reproducing assumptions about racial homogeneity and essentializing.

For example, one of the reasons why I chose to study basketball in my work on learning is because it is a common practice in the African American community. I do not, however, assume that all black people play basketball, although it can be conceptualized as a racialized practice, in that it is viewed in society as signaling African American racial group membership and identity. As another example, when I study African American racialized identity, I do make the assumption that such a thing as African American racialized identity exists and that it can be studied. Yet, I am careful to define the content of that identity as my research participants see it and to understand that there will be tremendous variation in what being African American means to people. I study race in a range of ways, from students' explicit articulation of what racial group membership means, to the ways that certain cultural practices are assumed to be aligned with particular racial groups.

This book addresses several critical gaps in the existing research literature and popular conversation about race, identity, and learning for African American students. First, the literature is abundant with descriptions of the identities and achievement of African American students when identity *does not* support learning (Fordham and Ogbu, 1986); however, we know less about what it looks like when identities and learning *are* aligned in schools or other cultural practices. I attempt to understand the nature of this alignment of social identity and learning and the characteristics of learning settings that foster it.

Second, current views of culture, race, and identity too often portray these as global, stable traits and less often highlight their local and fluid dimensions. I attend in this book to the local and fluid nature of culture, race, and identity, offering data and analyses that acknowledge change over time and over social spaces.

Third, current psychological measures of racial/ethnic identity often highlight the extent of racial group affiliation but do not explore variation with respect to what racialized identity *means* for people. A smaller set of studies does focus on the content of racialized identity but asks about the presence or absence of particular content, rather than understanding racialized identity from the perspective of the youth themselves (Sellers, Chavous, and Cooke, 1998; Shelton and Sellers, 2000). This work also falls short in acknowledging the ways that we, as a society, racialize (or make racial) certain identities in certain kinds of ways. In the chapters that follow, I pay particular attention to variations in racialized identities for youth and on how youth understand their racialized identities compared with their local settings, remembering that these racialized identities are *made* racial by our collective understandings of race.

Fourth, there is a shortage in the literature of contextualized accounts of racialized and academic identities in schools and classrooms—

that is, research that helps us understand the role of schools in supporting or not supporting particular identities (a notable exception to this is the work of Davidson [1996], which is more than ten years old). I not only examine the role of the local setting in making available particular configurations of racialized and academic identities, I also describe how these settings and the people in them accomplish this work.

And finally, there are few accounts of the role of stereotypes (or racial narratives) in students' racialized identities and of the connections between youths' endorsement of stereotypes and their academic achievement and learning. I explore this role and these connections.

It is my hope that this book contributes to the body of research on identity and learning for African American students and helps us better understand how learning and identity processes inform schooling and how they take shape as students engage a range of learning settings in and out of school.

Expanding the Conversation on African American Learners

In addition to enriching what we know about identities and their relation to learning, this book seeks to expand the conversation that currently dominates research on African American students. Too often, African American student learning and achievement is framed too simply as a problem of "achievement gaps" (Burris and Welner, 2005; Gutierrez, 2008; Ladson-Billings, 2006; Viadero and Johnston, 2001) or "oppositional identities" (Fordham and Ogbu, 1986; Tatum, 1992). When framed as a problem of achievement gaps, researchers most often ask, Why are the black kids achieving less well than the white (or Asian) kids? This question has led to a range of answers, from Eurocentric and deficit-oriented theories about African American families and communities to indictments of core inequalities in schools and society (Darling-Hammond, 2000; Grubb and Lazerson, 2004; Haycock, 1998; Ladson-Billings, 2006). When framed as a problem of oppositional identities, researchers ask, To what extent do the black kids have identities by which they define school as "white" or themselves as not students? In search of answers to this question, researchers have studied the ways African American students think about themselves and school and have articulated challenges with developing strong racial and academic identities (Carter, 2008; Graham, Taylor, and Hudley, 1998; Mikelson and Velasco, 2006; Morghan and Mehta, 2004; Osbourne, 1997; Tyson, Daroty, and Castellino, 2005). Research on African American students has largely been limited to these two framings.

At one level these framings are informative and useful, but limiting our inquiry to these two lenses is problematic because they both perpetuate what Perry (2003) and Martin (2009) have argued is a "master-narrative" about African American students in both scholarly and popular writing about education and race. By master-narrative, they mean the "dominant stories told by those in power from positions of privilege" that exist in the broader society (Martin, 2009, 8). That is, neither of these ways of framing African American student learning and achievement challenges the ways that our society thinks about and defines blackness— including viewing blackness as oppositional to whiteness and viewing African American students as not intellectually capable and not culturally prepared for achievement. Akom (2008), Lee (2008), and Spencer (2008) remind us that implicit in these portrayals of blackness are longstanding and deeply held hegemonic and normative beliefs about whiteness. And the vast literature on racial stereotypes confirms these aspects of the master-narrative regarding African American students (Devine and Elliott, 1995; Krueger, 1996; Hudley and Graham, 2001).

In this book, I attempt to offer a different angle on the issues facing African American students and their communities with respect to education by highlighting processes of identity and exploring the variety of ways they play out in and across learning settings. I do not adopt a frame that compares black students with white students, with white students representing the norm. I do not view African American students or their communities as problems. But perhaps most important, I hope to challenge in multiple ways common assumptions about African American students and the overwhelming focus in research on individual students' pathology rather than on the ways that our society organizes for the success of some and the failure of others (Varenne and McDermott, 1998).

Although clearly this book is about African American students, I don't view it as being *just* about African American students; rather, I am using African American students as a case with which to explore core questions about the nature of identity, the fundamental ways that identities are linked to social contexts, and the implications of these links for teaching and creating optimal learning environments.

In the chapters that follow, I draw on data from students who have found success in school and students who have not. However, rather than focus on the individual characteristics or adaptations that make students more or less successful, I focus on the organization of learning environments and the ways in which settings create more or less access to identities as learners. I take as central how broader societal institutions, norms, and structures come into play in relation to access to learning settings and identities as learners. Thus, this book wrestles with several critical questions:

- How can we understand the relation between processes of learning and processes of identity? How are identities and learning related for African American students as they take part in school and/or community-based learning settings?

- How do learning settings make identities available to students, and how are certain identities made available and not others?

- What role do racialized identities play in engagement in school learning settings for African American students, and how can we conceptualize these racialized identities in ways that are not oversimplified or essentialized?

Through addressing these questions, I hope to contribute to our conceptual understanding of learning and identity processes as being linked in fundamental ways to culture and context. I also hope to add to the conversation on the relation between identities and achievement for African American students and deeply consider what resources local contexts offer as students seek to learn and to establish a sense of self.

I rely on qualitative accounts of identity in this book; that is, I discuss identity by drawing primarily on interview, observational, and case study data. I do so largely because qualitative data support the portrayal of the kind of nuance and complexity of identities and learning that I hope to describe.

Overview of the Text

Chapter 1 lays the theoretical groundwork and guiding assumptions of this book and orients the reader to the scholarly conversation to which this book seeks to contribute. Chapter 2 describes interactions between learning and identity processes in learning settings outside of school and highlights the ways in which these settings provide resources for learning identities to African American youth. I also consider the relationship between racialized identities and learning in these spaces.

Chapter 3 is the first of three chapters that take up the relation between engagement and achievement in school and students' racialized identities. In it I explore students' perspectives on what it means to be African American, attending to the contradictions and complexities in their conceptions of race and racialized identity. I also attend to how they talk about stereotypes in relation to blackness. In Chapter 4, I describe two very different configurations of the relation between racialized identities and academic identities and explore how the school context supports each. In Chapter 5, I examine the racialized and academic identity configurations of students who are in the midst of managing multiple conflicting racialized and academic identities, illustrating the complexity and multifaceted nature of identity.

Chapter 6 highlights important themes across the previous chapters, including the linking of learning to students' developing social identities, the ways that identities and learning processes support one another as young people participate in social and cultural activities, and the complexity of racialized identities and the ways they interact with learning identities. Finally, Chapter 7 considers the implications of this work for classroom teachers and articulates several important lessons for teaching practice, interactions with students, and the design of learning environments.

I hope that this book comes close to doing justice to the full humanity and perspectives of the students whom I have studied and that it contributes to the scholarly conversation about race, learning, and identity. I also hope my research and perspectives foster a conversation in the field that honors the complexity of identity processes and their relation to learning and acknowledges the ways that we, as a society, fail to develop the potential of so many African American youth as we perpetuate debilitating stereotypes about who they can become. Furthermore, I hope this book serves as a call for more people to attend to the multiple ways that race influences the learning experiences and outcomes of African American youth and to take up the formidable challenge of providing positive, supportive, enriching learning spaces for young people.

Note

1. Throughout this book, I use the terms "African American" and "black" interchangeably.

1

Identity as Possibility and Limitation

VICTOR WAS ONE OF THOSE STUDENTS who defied categorization—and he liked it that way. He was a tall, medium-brown-skinned, African American young man, his hair twisted into the beginnings of dreadlocks, with a ready smile. Victor was a charmer, so he always made our mostly female research team feel welcomed. He had big ideas; Victor was a theoretical thinker, who expressed pride in his academic accomplishments and delivered stinging critiques of the educational and social systems that he saw as perpetuating inequality. He had a wide range of friends—both students who were leaders in the school and high academic achievers, and students who barely went to class and smoked marijuana to get through the school day. He was smart, but he often chatted with his friends rather than participate in class.

When we first got to know Victor, in his junior year, he was considered one of the school's top students. He had represented the school at a national student government meeting in Washington, D.C., and was enrolled in advanced placement (AP) history. He planned to attend college. By his senior year, however, Victor had failed several classes, his attendance was spotty, and he doubted the relevance of college to his life. When asked about his declining performance, Victor noted that he was tired of struggling against the perceptions society and other people had of him. He spoke candidly about his effort to craft a sense of who he was racially. He felt that his peers and the world expected him to be "gangster" and "hard," to dress a certain way and to listen to a certain type of music. Yet the persona they expected did not feel authentic to him.

Victor was hamstrung both by a system he felt was rigged and by the challenge of figuring out who he was when the messages that he had to be hard were all too prevalent. His identity as a student and as an African American male were limited by the ideas he perceived in the world around him, with severe consequences for both his educational trajectory and his identity.

The idea that the racialized structure of our society and the prevalence of discrimination (in multiple forms) matters for the identities of African American and other minority students is not a new one. Indeed, it dates back to at least the 1930s, when Kenneth Clark conducted the first racial identity studies with black and white children by measuring students' preferences for black and white dolls (Clark and Clark, 1939). For African American students the relation between racial identity and school achievement is still very much in the forefront in both lay and scholarly conversations about school achievement and learning. Theories of "oppositional identities" (Fordham and Ogbu, 1986; O'Connor, Horvat, and Lewis, 2006; Ogbu, 1987, 1992) dominate the research literature on African American students and debates about race and schooling in the United States. These theories purport that African American students see school as associated with being white and thus *disidentify* with school in an effort to preserve their blackness. However, to argue that Victor has an oppositional identity with respect to school doesn't capture the nuances and complexities of the self he constructs in relation to the school and neighborhood contexts that he navigates.

Victor's struggle illustrates a fundamental developmental challenge for all young people in our society; that is, they must construct a sense of identity that incorporates their experiences and perceptions from the multiple settings in which they engage. This integration has implications for their motivation to engage in formal learning settings, and for their educational and life trajectories. However, this identity work is historically situated. The ideas about what it means to be African American and a student that Victor feels the world asks him to respond to run counter to a long tradition in the African American community of viewing education as integral to racial progress.

The Legacy of Schooling as Identity Work in African American Education

The connection between education and identity has long been attended to in the African American community. The historical record speaks to the fervor with which enslaved Africans, and later newly freed slaves, sought to learn to read and write; this intense desire to learn was tied to a sense that education was an avenue through which one could nurture and actualize human potential. That is, through education one could engage in society more centrally, be viewed as a full human being with rights and privileges, and have greater access to determining one's future—one could *become* a new kind of person. Anderson (1988) recounts the zeal with which African Americans sought out education after the Emancipation Proclamation of 1863, when black ex-slaves looked to education to disrupt social and economic inequality. He quotes Harriet Beecher Stowe speaking in 1865 of the recent ex-slaves: "They rushed not to the grog-shop, but to the schoolroom—they cried for the spelling book as bread and teachers as a necessity of life" (5). Anderson also quotes Booker T. Washington, speaking in 1900: "Few people who were not right in the midst of the scene can form any exact idea of the intense desire which the people of my race showed for education. It was a whole race trying to go to school. Few were too young and none too old to make an attempt to learn" (5).

It is clear from these comments that learning and schooling were primary goals for newly freed ex-slaves. In 1894 Frederick Douglass also conveyed in a speech this burning desire for learning and highlighted how learning and schooling were tied to issues of identity and personhood for ex-slaves:

> But if man is without education although with all his latent possibility attaching to him he is, as I have said, but a pitiable object; a giant in body but a pigmy in intellect, and at best but half a man. Without education he lives within the narrow, dark and grimy walls of ignorance. He is a poor prisoner without hope. The little light that he gets comes to him as through dark corridors and grated windows. The sights and sounds that reach him, so significant and full of meaning to the well trained mind, are to him of dim and shadowy importance. He sees,

but does not perceive. He hears, but does not understand. The silent and majestic heavens fretted with stars, so inspiring and uplifting, so sublime and glorious to the souls of other men, bear no message to him. They suggest to him no idea of the wonderful world in which we live, or of the harmony of this great universe, and hence, impart to him no happiness.

Education, on the other hand, means emancipation. It means light and liberty. It means the uplifting of the soul of man into the glorious light of truth, the light by which men can only be made free. To deny education to any people is one of the greatest crimes against human nature. It is easy to deny them the means of freedom and the rightful pursuit of happiness and to defeat the very end of their being. They can neither honor themselves nor their Creator. Than this, no greater wrong can be inflicted; and, on the other hand, no greater benefit can be bestowed upon a long benighted people, than giving to them, as we are here earnestly this day endeavoring to do, the means of an education. (Douglass, 1894)

Scholars and historians have highlighted the importance of learning for enslaved Africans, even as they risked severe punishment and death to pursue it. This seeking of education was not just about gaining access to material resources; it was also about being seen as fully human, as an educated person. Implicit in Douglass's speech is an appeal that African Americans be viewed as full humans, and Douglass's status as an educated man is central in that appeal. The connection between humanity and education was very much about identity—with respect to both how African Americans viewed themselves (as upstanding citizens who sought out opportunities to be educated) and how they were viewed by white Americans.

In the African American tradition, schools and education have played two roles with respect to identity. The first is an inward role that involves supporting African American youth in conceptualizing themselves both as members of a strong, resilient people with much to contribute to this country, and as potential scholars, academics, and powerful students. The second is an outward role, whereby being educated tells others something about who African Americans are and speaks to the potential in African Americans as a people (and at the same time speaks to the atrocities of enslavement and oppression).

Issues of identity and learning are deeply tied to the idea, articulated by Douglass, of realizing full humanity through education. At its best, education should involve helping one to actualize one's innate potential and to become equipped to enact one's unique contribution to society and the world. W. E. B. Du Bois (1903), in a statement about black colleges, speaks to the complex mission, involving identity, of education for African Americans:

> The function of the Negro college, thus, is clear: it must maintain the standards of popular education, it must seek the social regeneration of the Negro, and it must help the solution of problems of race contact and cooperation. And finally, beyond all of this, it must develop men. Above our modern socialism, and out of the worship of the mass, must persist and evolve that higher individualism which centers of culture protect; there must come a loftier respect for the sovereign human soul that seeks to know itself and the world about it. (66)

Du Bois makes the case that the role of the Negro college is both about supporting learning and social uplift and about developing men (and presumably women) to know themselves and the world around them. He reiterates the point that the goals of educating young people and helping them better understand who they are and how they fit into the world are critical to supporting the learning and development of African Americans.

Thus the connection between education and identity has a long history in the struggle for African American education; this historical context is an important counter to current conceptualizations of African American identity being in opposition to schooling. I find it fascinating that the current struggles and debates regarding education and identity in the African American community, set in a climate of increasing disparity in access to educational resources, resonate in many ways with similar tensions and debates in the early part of the twentieth century. And yet, clearly, there are also aspects of how we think about African American identity, and how that relates to educational and identity processes, that are rooted in the ideologies and practices of the current time.

Defining Learning and Identity

It is important to be precise about my use of the terms "learning" and "identity" because in the recent literature on learning and identities, scholars have argued for the interrelationship of these two processes (Nasir and Cooks, 2009; Wenger, 1998). Since these processes are viewed as having implications for one another, I need to be clear about how I am defining them in distinct ways.

By *learning* I mean shifts in ways of understanding, thinking about concepts, and solving problems and closely related shifts in ways of doing or participating in activities. Current perspectives on learning view it as involving not simply transmission from the teacher to the learner (as a behaviorist perspective would view learning), but as involving cognitive processes of problem-solving, transfer, reflection, prior knowledge, and the development of expertise (Bransford, Brown, and Cocking, 2000; Sawyer, 2006). Scholarship over the past ten years has also highlighted how, in addition to involving cognitive processing, learning is deeply intertwined with social processes and ways of participating in learning activities (Bransford, Brown, and Cocking, 2000; Greeno, 2006; Lave and Wenger, 1991). This work has highlighted the fact that learning always involves an interplay between individual cognition and a socially and culturally organized learning setting, where learning is, in part, indexed by changing relations between people and increasingly sophisticated use of available tools for problem-solving.

By *identity* I mean a sense of self, constructed from available social categories, taken up by individuals and ascribed by cultural groups and social settings. This definition builds on symbolic interactionism (Goffman, 1959; Mead, 1934), sociocultural perspectives (Holland et al., 1998; Wenger, 1998), sociological perspectives (Stryker, 1987), and developmental psychology approaches (Erikson, 1959, 1968; Marica, 1966, 1980). Identity is a concept that also captures the interplay between social and cultural institutions and norms, and individual learning and developmental trajectories. Identities take shape as a part of a cultural process of becoming—a becoming that is guided by our ever-evolving sense of who we are and who we can be.

These definitions preserve the distinction between processes of learning and processes of identity and define each in ways that honor the culturally bound and context-dependent nature of each.

Guiding Assumptions

My exploration of learning and identity processes is guided by several critical assumptions that form a foundation, of sorts, upon which the data in the following chapters build:

- Although learning and identity processes deeply inform one another, they are conceptually distinct.

- Learning and identity are always cultural and social processes, linked in fundamental ways to the contexts in which they occur.

- Racialized identities are important to consider in a highly racially stratified society such as that in the United States, where strong and long-held racial stereotypes exist, as well as tremendous racial disparities in all aspects of society.

- Racialized identities are related to the complex process of racial socialization, which occurs in family and school contexts.

- Identities, including racialized identities, are fluid and shift in relation to setting, salience, and local definitions and opportunities.

Each of these guiding assumptions serves as an orientation to the data that follow and situate the core concerns in this book in relation to several relevant strands in the research literature. In the following pages, I describe in more detail each assumption and draw on relevant research and theory.

Although learning and identity are processes that deeply inform one another, they are conceptually distinct. There has been much theorizing from a sociocultural perspective about the implications that learning and identity have for one another (Boaler and Greeno, 2000; Lave and Wenger, 1991; Wenger, 1998; Wortham, 2006). For instance, Wenger (1998) conceptualizes learning as an aspect of identity and identity as a result of learning. For Wenger, both learning and identity have to do with shifting relationships to people and objects in a particular setting and involve membership in communities of practice. This perspective reconceptualizes learning from an in-the-head phenomenon to a matter of engagement, participation, and membership in a community of practice, and engages in a substantive discussion on relations between identity and learning in practices.

Research on the learning and achievement of minority students has also highlighted (or implied) the relation between learning processes and identity processes (Conchas, 2001; Fordham and Ogbu, 1986; Levinson, Foley, and Holland, 1996; Mehan, 1996; Ogbu, 1987; Osbourne, 1997) and has noted the powerful role that the social context plays in which identities are made available to whom—identities that can constrain or enable opportunities for learning and success in school (Davidson, 1996; Ferguson, 2000; McDermott and Varenne, 1995). However, we must also be clear about the conceptual distinctions between learning processes and identity processes. One example of research that makes this distinction is the work of Boaler (1999) and Boaler and Greeno (2000). In a study of reform and traditional math classes they explored how students' identities as mathematics learners varied with the structure of the classroom, the curriculum, and the nature of the mathematical tasks that students were required to perform. These researchers argue that the ability of students to do the math is not by itself enough to support strong mathematical identities; rather, mathematical identities are tied to understanding and engaging authentic involvement in mathematics and students being able to see themselves as effective mathematics learners in the classroom. In other words, students can master the practices of the traditional mathematics classroom and learn the math competently without taking on the identity of themselves as mathematical thinkers or "math people." Thus, these researchers argue for the distinction between processes of learning and processes of identity. Similarly, Herrenkohl and Wertsch (1999) distinguish between mastery (akin to learning) and appropriation (akin to identity). In their view, one can master skills without appropriating them. The theoretical task at hand, then, is to understand with greater nuance the relations between learning and identity processes, while also preserving their conceptual distinctions.

Learning and identity development are always cultural and social processes, linked in fundamental ways to the contexts in which they occur. Research in the sociocultural (Cole, 1996; Engestrom, 1999; Rogoff, 2003; Wenger,

1998) and ecological (Bronfenbrenner, 1979, 1993; Lerner, 1991; Spencer, 2006) traditions supports a view of identity and learning as being deeply informed by social context. In these theories, social context influences learning and identity through the organization of activities in which people participate and through the values, norms, and expectations conveyed in those activities (Nasir, 2004). For example, in the cultural practice of basketball, learning happens as players work together to improve their game and engage in practices structured by the coach and high-stakes performances in games. In game play, it is expected that players will play certain positions or roles, and one norm is that players receive extensive in-the-moment feedback on their play.

Social context includes both immediate contexts, such as homes or classrooms, and more distal contexts, such as institutions and society (Bronfenbrenner, 1993). Many have noted the multilayered quality of context, which can be conceptualized as a set of concentric circles made up of increasingly broad levels of context (Bronfenbrenner, 1979; Lewin, 1935; Cole, 1996); this idea that context is multilayered and deeply influences individuals has a long history in the scholarly literature (Bourdieu, 1977; Bronfenbrenner, 1979, 1986; Cole, 1996; Lewin, 1935, 1951; Ogbu, 1987; Vygotsky, 1978; Gallimore, Goldenberg, and Weisner, 1993).

Learning and identity processes are situated within cultural practices (Cole, 1996; Saxe, 1999; Wenger, 1998), which are defined as reoccurring, goal-directed activities that involve two or more people (Saxe, 1999). Examples of cultural practices include eating dinner at the family dinner table, playing games, standing in line at the grocery store, or engaging in a school lesson on algebra.

A focus on cultural practices is grounded in a theoretical perspective that sees such practices as a critical aspect of culture. The cultural-practice view sees culture as lived, locally constituted, and fluid, consisting of activities, tools, social others, and ways of organizing a routine (Cole, 1996; Gutiérrez and Rogoff, 2003; Lee, 2007). This definition encompasses what Gutiérrez and Rogoff (2003) refer to as "repertoires of practice," by which they mean "the ways of engaging in activities stemming from observing and otherwise participating in cultural practices" (22).

A cultural-practice view of culture also has implications for where we look as researchers when we study learning. Building on the theories of Russian psychologists Vygotsky (1962, 1978) and Leontiev (1978), research from this perspective takes as a core unit of analysis the cultural practices that people engage in as they go about their daily lives. From a practice perspective, learning and identity are as much about shifts in participation in social and cultural practices and activities as about shifts in ways of thinking (Lave and Wenger, 1991; Rogoff, 1993, 2003).

Cultural practices are composed of individuals and are set within institutions and societies. For instance, a classroom lesson on algebra is set within a particular institution of schooling with its own history, purposes, and norms. Institutions are set within societies, which also have norms and ideologies. Or, take the case of Victor from the beginning of this chapter. His struggles around identity were linked in important ways to the local school context, which had a history of underachievement and poor resources for learning but which was actively trying to "grow" a cohort of high achievers. His struggles were also linked to the broader society that tended to structure educational resources on the basis of race and which gave rise to the resource-poor urban neighborhood in which Victor lived.

Thus, context is fundamentally related to learning and identity in several ways. Both learning and identity occur in culturally organized activities (whether this be school or neighborhood games), involve social artifacts (computers, toys, pencils, uniforms), happen in the presence of and through interaction with others (peers, teachers, coaches, elders, family members), are guided by social norms (about what is optimal, right, good), and are engaged in as individuals seek to attain socially constructed goals (to get good grades, to win, to support one's family, to connect socially with others).

This perspective suggests that any study of identity and learning must also include an examination of the nature of the context within which learning and identity take place and offers suggestions about ways to understand how these contextual influences play out.

Racialized identities are important to consider in a racially stratified society such as that in the United States, where strong and long-held racial stereotypes exist, as well as tremendous racial disparities in all aspects of society. In conceptualizing race, I draw on Omi and Winant (1994) to define race as "a concept which signifies and symbolizes social conflicts and interests by referring to different types of human bodies" (55). Note that this definition largely views race as a social phenomenon and not as a biological one. The American Anthropological Association (1998) writes, "The 'racial' worldview was invented to assign some groups to perpetual low status, while others were permitted access to privilege, power, and wealth." Perhaps because of this underlying issue of access to power, talking about race is difficult (both in the world and in the academy).[1] These definitions bring to the fore the ways in which race is employed in the service of the establishment and maintenance of power relations in society.

One important way that race and ideas about race contribute to the maintenance of a racial hierarchy in the United States is by influencing the ways that individual members of racial groups see themselves and their place in society through the perpetuation of *stereotypes* that also may inform the development of racial identity (Bobo, 2001). Stereotypes can be defined as "mental representations of the characteristics of a particular social or cultural group that are shared among members of society" (from Stangor and Schaller, 1996, cited in Hudley and Graham, 2001, 202). A large body of research confirms the prevalence of racial stereotypes, and strong and longstanding cultural stereotypes exist about African American youth. African Americans are assumed to have low intelligence, to lack an achievement orientation, and to engage in antisocial behavior (Devine and Elliott, 1995; Krueger, 1996; Hudley and Graham, 2001). More recently, contemporary stereotypes of African American (primarily male) youth have been tied to media portrayals of African American men as thugs and gangsters (Bailey, 2006; Chan, 2005; Dance, 2002; Deburg, 2004), and some researchers have highlighted the role of hip-hop and rap music in perpetuating these images (Rome, 2004). Research has shown that even young children have some understanding of the stereotypes that exist about their own and other racial groups (McKown and Weinstein, 2003; Van Ausdale and Feagin, 2001) and that adolescents are highly aware of such stereotypes (Hudley and Graham, 2001).

Steele and colleagues (Steele, 1997, 1998; Steele and Aronson, 1995) have demonstrated the power of racial and gender stereotypes with respect to achievement in stereotyped domains (for instance, women in math or African American students in standardized test settings). These studies show that when students in a stereotyped group (with respect to a particular domain) believe a test to be diagnostic in that domain or when they are asked to record their race before testing, their performance suffers because of anxiety produced by the fear of confirming a negative stereotype about their group. Steele and colleagues have called this phenomenon *stereotype threat*. Work on stereotype threat brings to the fore the socially held and shared stereotypes about various social groups and the effect of such stereotypes on academic outcomes. This work highlights two important points: first, stereotypes about race are broadly held and socially shared, and second, such stereotypes influence individual learning and, potentially, academic trajectories.

And yet, we also know that stereotypes are filtered—both by the nature of the local contexts that students are negotiating and by students' individual sense-making processes. That is, not every student subscribes to a stereotypical representation of himself or herself with respect to race. This is evident in my own work (Nasir, Jones, and McLaughlin, 2009) and in the work of others (Carter, 2008; Carter, 2005; Davidson, 1996; Sanders, 1997). Research has shown that students' conceptions of race and its relation to school vary significantly. Research has also highlighted individual differences in students' vulnerability to stereotypes and success in navigating them (Crocker and Major, 1989; Oyserman et al., 2003). Often, these locally constituted notions on the part of students share some characteristics across localities, but they play out differently and shift in multiple ways in relation to the social and cultural context (of the school and community).

Racial stereotypes are likely related to *racialized identity*, in that stereotypes provide possible content for the racialized identities that young people are in the process of developing.[2] In other words, when young people ask the question, What does it mean to be African American?, the world provides a set of answers rooted in long-held stereotypes about African Americans.

In schools, academic identities can be problematic for many African American students, in part, researchers argue, because they conflict with students' definitions of what it means to be a member of their racial group (Davidson, 1996; Fordham and Ogbu, 1986; Spencer, 1987, 1999). One influential theory in this regard has been Fordham and Ogbu's "acting white" hypothesis (Fordham, 1991, 1996; Fordham and Ogbu, 1986).

This argument posits that because African American youth view school achievement as a "white" phenomenon, they take one of three possible positions. Some choose not to invest in school (in order to preserve their perceptions of "blackness"); others choose to become "raceless" in order to engage and achieve in school; still others take up oppositional identities to preserve their sense of racial group membership. This theory has been highly controversial in the field and has given rise to a myriad of responses and refinements (see, for example, Carter, 2005; Mikelson and Velasco, 2006; Tyson, Daroty, and Castellino, 2005).

One point that has been hotly contested is the idea that students associate school achievement with whiteness; research has both confirmed and disconfirmed this hypothesis. Graham, Taylor, and Hudley (1998) used peer nominations of male and female African American and Latino adolescents as a proxy for the extent to which students valued doing well in school. They found an interaction between race and gender which showed that most students nominated peers who were both academically and socially successful, while African American boys tended to nominate students who were not academically successful. Thus, for many students, achieving in school did not seem to be stigmatized as antiblack or undesirable for black students, but for some students (African American boys, in particular), doing well in school did seem to be less valued. Osbourne (1997) reports similar findings.

However, since its inception, scholars have argued against the idea of an oppositional identity and have highlighted how African Americans respond to racism and discrimination in ways that promote academic success. Both the historical record and current research support this position. Anderson (1988) contends that African Americans have historically possessed a strong achievement orientation that has resulted in a solid collective struggle for quality education. Research has suggested that African Americans are connected to the dominant achievement ideology (Ainsworth-Darnell and Downey, 1998; O'Connor, 1997) and do not disidentify with doing well in school (Morgan and Mehta, 2004) or education in general. Ainsworth-Darnell and Downey (1998) used data from a national survey and found that African Americans do not perceive a limited opportunity structure more often than white Americans. Moreover, they reported that among African American students, those with more positive attitudes toward school and higher achievement were seen as popular. These findings challenge the claim that African Americans hold oppositional identities and that these identities are required for within-group status.

O'Connor (1997) argues that the oppositional identity argument does not account for the variation in how African American students give meaning to, interpret, and respond to the opportunity structures afforded to them. Furthermore, research has illustrated that some African American students succeed academically and possess a black cultural frame of reference that sustains ties to their communities (Carter, 2008; Carter, 2005; Moody, 2004; Stinson, 2008).

Undoubtedly, the nature of African American students' racialized identities has profound implications for their sense of self in the world and in school. Yet, we have only begun to explore the variety of ways that students construct and make sense of their racialized selves and their sense of themselves as students, the ways that they make sense of the role of school in their lives, and the ways that they navigate the myriad of stereotypes about them both in school and in society at large.

Additionally, the body of research on racialized identities for African American students too often fails to acknowledge the fluidity and constructed nature of racialized identities and the ways certain identities are *made* racial by a society that makes sense of them as such. Along these lines, Bobo (1999) (summarizing Blumer's theory of social positioning) writes, "Racial identities are quasi-autonomous social forces, ranking with economic and other institutional dynamics in shaping human social organization" (450). Blumer (by way of Bobo) describes the interplay between racial(ized) identities and the social world of which they are a part—arguing that racial(ized) identities themselves become a social force that shapes social organization.

Racialized identities are related to the complex process of racial socialization, which occurs in family and school contexts. Racialized identities emerge in relation to exposure to various forms of racial socialization, both in families and in school settings. Miller (1999) has argued that processes of racial socialization and racial identities are "inextricably bound," since racial socialization is a factor in the nature and development of one's racial(ized) identity and "racial socialization is influenced by the racial identity of the family" (497). In other words, racial identities are constructed as individuals interact with others in a racially stratified world, but the beliefs one holds about race, and the ways that one responds to instances of racism, are related to the messages relayed by families and schools about race and racism.

Most of the research on racial socialization examines the messages about race and navigating racism that occur in the context of *families*, specifically between parents and children (Bowman and Howard, 1985; Hughes and Johnson, 2001; Hughes et al., 2006; Miller, 1999). Racial socialization is defined as the "mechanisms through which parents transmit information, values, and perspectives about ethnicity and race" (Hughes et al., 2006, 747). These messages about race vary in nature; the literature has identified four key types of information about race conveyed in families: cultural socialization, preparation for bias, promotion of mistrust, and egalitarianism or color blindness (Hughes et al., 2006; Hughes and Chen, 1997). Boykin and Toms (1985) argue that these types of information are related to the fact that parents of African American children are engaging in multiple tasks in this racial socialization work, including preparing young people for engagement in mainstream society, preparing them for the experience of being a member of a cultural minority, and socializing them into membership in the cultural community of African Americans.

Cultural socialization refers to the messages that parents transmit about their heritage and racial/ethnic history. This includes parental practices such as telling stories about historical figures in African and African American history and engaging in cultural activities. It also includes the presence of cultural artifacts, such as African or African American art (Marshall, 1995). Cultural socialization messages are the most common form of racial socialization (Hughes et al., 2006), and they are related to positive outcomes such as positive racial/ethnic identity (Demo and Hughes, 1990; Marshall, 1995; O'Connor, Brooks-Gunn, and Graber, 2000), higher self-esteem (Constantine and Blackmon, 2002), and fewer behavioral problems (Caughy et al., 2002).

Preparation for bias, the next most common form of racial socialization (Hughes et al., 2006), often occurs in response to an incident of discrimination or racism and offers young people strategies for coping with and responding to racial discrimination (Bowman and Howard, 1985; Hughes et al., 2006; Thornton et al., 1990). This form of racial socialization has also been found to have positive effects on youth outcomes, including high self-esteem (Constantine and Blackmon, 2002) and increased ability to cope with prejudice and discrimination (Johnson, 1994; Scott, 2003).

Promotion of mistrust refers to racial socialization messages which convey that mainstream people and institutions are racist and promote discriminatory practices (Hughes et al., 2006; Hughes and Chen, 1997). Research on the outcomes related to promotion of mistrust strategies is less developed but seems to indicate that promotion of mistrust messages tend to have a negative effect on self-esteem and academic outcomes (Hughes et al., 2006). It may be that simply pointing out the pervasive presence of racism, without suggestions about how one might cope with discrimination, can be overwhelming and promote depression and negative coping strategies (Rumbaut, 1994).

The final form of racial socialization discussed in the literature, *egalitarianism or color blindness*, downplays the importance of race, instead promoting "mainstream socialization" (Boykin and Toms, 1985) and hard work, virtue, and equality (Demo and Hughes, 1990; Hughes et al., 2006; Marshall, 1995). Color blindness or silence about race includes not discussing or minimizing the salience of race and racism. By and large, these types of racial socialization tend to be less effective (and even harmful) with respect to both social and academic outcomes (Hughes et al., 2006).

Thus, the research on racial socialization has documented several distinct categories of racial socialization practices, and findings have demonstrated that when young people are encouraged to think positively about their own racial/ethnic group, and are offered support in optimal ways of coping with discrimination, they develop positive racial(ized) identities and are more likely to find successful ways to cope and have better academic and social outcomes. When parents promote racial mistrust of other people and of institutions, or when they downplay the importance of race, outcomes are less favorable.

Although not generally referred to as studies of racial socialization, there is a small body of research on the types of messages about race and racism that children and adolescents tend to encounter in *schools* (Lewis, 2003; Pollock, 2005; Skinner and Schafer, 2009). Research in this genre has tended to rely on qualitative and observational methods to examine the nuances and complexities of the messages about race conveyed in schools. For instance, Skinner and Schafer (2009) focus on the maintenance of racial boundaries in an elementary school classroom, documenting how race is invoked and deployed in interactions between students in ways that reify and maintain racial boundaries. Lewis (2003) also takes up the issue of how people talk about and construct racial categories, as well as how schools are organized in ways that maintain the racial privilege of white students and parents while maintaining a discourse of diversity. She compares messages about race conveyed in three elementary schools with varying student populations and orientations to issues of race. Her findings show that while schools vary significantly in the extent to which they explicitly discuss or address issues of race, racial boundaries are maintained and conveyed to even young students in all of the schools that she studied.

Research has also documented racial socialization processes in the context of high schools (Nasir, Jones, and McLaughlin, 2009; Pollock, 2005). For example, Pollock (2005) studied racial discourse and racial sense-making in a diverse urban public high school. Her findings showed that although teachers and administrators were reluctant to talk about race (a phenomenon she calls being "colormute"), students were developing a racialized sense of the school social networks and their place in them. Much like the color-blind racial socialization strategies, these policies and practices on the part of the school tended to re-create racial hierarchies and leave students poorly equipped to name and cope with the racism they encountered in the school context.

In all of these studies, researchers describe the prevalence of students' narratives about race and about what it means to belong to one race or another. Often, these narratives reinforce existing societal stereotypes about racial groups, and as students, teachers, and administrators enact these narratives, racist and discriminatory practices in schools are maintained and reified.

Identities, including racial identities, are fluid and shift in relation to setting, salience, and local definitions and opportunities. In some theoretical approaches, identity has been conceptualized as static, located within individuals, and as something they carry around inside of them. I argue that identity does optimally have some stable characteristics, but it is also shaped in core ways by the multiple contexts that individuals navigate in their daily lives (Cooley, 1922; Holland et al., 1998; Mead, 1934; Wenger, 1998). As we engage in learning settings, our identities are constructed through expectations, the availability of roles, social interactions with others, and norms. Furthermore, identity is rooted in experiences in social settings and yet also transcends these local settings, linking youth across multiple settings and being conveyed through media outlets, such as music, television, and movies. This is true of African American racialized identity (and racialized white identity, too, for that matter), which is transmitted in the practices of families and communities, but also in the mass media. Such a perspective draws on both sociocultural theory and sociological accounts of identity in the work of Stryker (1987) and is reminiscent of early accounts of the social and interactive dimensions of identity in the work of Mead (1934) and Goffman (1959, 1963, 1974).

Racialized identities have also historically been studied as properties of individuals, though it has been acknowledged that these individual processes are rooted in historical and community processes (Cross, 1991; Helms, 1990; Tatum, 1997). Local and interactional processes also influence the development of racialized identity at the level of cultural practices. For instance, as students engage in interactions with their peer groups at school, peers may convey messages about what racial group membership means in that setting and what versions of such racial identity are valued. As another example, certain games or other historical practices may be associated with particular race or class groups, and thus participation in them may signal racial group membership (Nasir and Saxe, 2003).

The identities that individuals construct within cultural practices are also deeply interwoven with sociohistorical notions of race and stereotypes that exist in contemporary American society. These societal conceptions constitute ideas (which have been termed "ideational artifacts"; see Nasir, 2004, and Cole, 1996) that get taken up and acted upon in local settings. Historical time also shifts the possibilities for who one can become. Clearly, the possibilities for what it meant to be African American in the 1950s were quite different from those of today. Indeed, heated debates over the term that should be used to refer to African Americans in this country have occurred every twenty years or so (from "colored" to "black" to "Afro-American" to "African American"), and underlying these debates are assumptions and values around what it means to be African American.

It is also important to understand contemporary African American youths' racialized identities given the shifting national climate around race (in a post–affirmative action era), where conversations about race are decreasingly explicit (Pollock, 2005). Furthermore, at the same time that issues of race have become less explicit, youth are exposed at unprecedented levels to an increasingly globalized media culture (Goodman and Dretzin, 2001), which blurs the lines between racial groups yet profits from gangster stereotypes of African Americans (Jhally, 1997; Ro, 1996).

Media portrayals of African Americans must be understood as part of a long history of racism, discrimination, and exploitation in the United States (Frederickson, 2002). The media have consistently offered a relatively narrow set of identity choices for nondominant people and youth in particular (Page, 1997). For African American youth, media images reinforce stereotypes of these groups as potentially dangerous, anti-intellectual, and downtrodden. As Essed (2002) argues, these racial images, by virtue of their repeated use, become "common-sense," thus making them both pervasive and insidious. Spencer (2006) has argued that the prevalence of stereotypes in the media has negative developmental consequences for African American students. As I have noted, other research has confirmed that adolescents (and even young children) understand stereotypes about their own and other groups (Baron and Banaji, 2006; Hudley and Graham, 2001; McKown and Weinstein, 2003). Thus, prevalent stereotypes about African American students and the ways those stereotypes are perceived by students may form an important part of the context that students negotiate (Steele, 1997).

A Focus on Variation

These guiding assumptions constitute a theoretical grounding for the chapters that follow. They also represent an effort to think purposefully about the role of culture and context in learning, identity, and educational processes. Some have argued that this attention to culture and context is necessary as scholars work to evolve the field of the learning sciences into one that offers conceptual tools to help us better understand variation in learning and educational outcomes, rather than a learning science that perceives there to be only one optimal pathway and outcome (O'Conner and Penuel, 2010). I view this book as working to advance this kind of nuanced understanding of learning and learning settings by focusing on issues of identity in learning and schooling contexts for African American students. As I engage this task, I am fundamentally concerned with accounting for and understanding variation in learning and identity processes.

Throughout this book, I explore variations in learning, schooling, and identities for African American students in two ways. I begin by focusing on the relation between identities and learning in learning settings outside of school—in community and after-school settings, where in the specific contexts that I studied, racialized identities were not viewed to be a problem for learning. I then turn to a focus on learning and identities in school contexts, examining cases in which social identities and schooling/learning processes seem to support one another, cases in which they clearly do not support one another, and cases in which the complexities and contradictions of student identities come to the fore as students struggle to juggle multiple and potentially conflicting identities. Thus, I examine both variation between settings and variation within school settings.

Notes

1. I would also note that race is related to culture in that cultural membership is based on shared routine practices and beliefs that are transmitted through generations across time and space.

2. Here and in this section I primarily use the term "racialized" identities, though much of the work I review uses the term "racial" identities.

2

When Learning and Identities Align

OCTAVIA WAS A SOPHOMORE when she got involved in track and field, and she didn't identify as an athlete at all. She joined the track team only because her mother required it (her brother also ran track, so it made picking up the children after school more convenient, and her mother thought Octavia needed to occupy her time with something other than boys). And yet, at the end of the first season, she had learned the skill of hurdling and come to see herself as a hurdler. She participated in track meets, worked hard to improve her performance, and mentored the younger members of the team.

Many factors contributed to this outcome in Octavia's learning and identity at the season's end: she had access to ample learning resources, she was viewed as having potential as a hurdler, and she was under the tutelage of a coach who believed in creating spaces where students developed both as athletes and as adolescents. Octavia's story is an example of the possible strengths of out-of-school learning settings for supporting both the learning and identities of young people, and it illustrates the intertwining of learning and identity processes in learning settings. As Octavia came to see herself as a hurdler, her commitment to the event intensified, and her persistence in learning moments increased. As she came to learn the expert practice of hurdling, her identity as a hurdler was strengthened.

The view of identities as locally constituted in local spaces leads to the question of how local cultural practices, whether they be community activities or classroom activities, support particular identities in youth. Research on learning in the community practices of marginalized communities is relevant here. Researchers have come to understand marginalized communities as places where young people learn important skills and develop knowledge bases (Yosso, 2005). For many students (even for those who fail in school), community activities are settings where they spend a significant amount of time (Larson and Verma, 1999; Larson et al., 2001) and learn quite effectively (Heath and McLaughlin, 1993; Lee, 1995, 2007; Moll and González, 2004; Lee and Majors, 2003; Majors, 2003; Ball and Brice-Heath, 1993). My own work on learning in the context of games and sports teams has confirmed these findings and has explored the ways activities in community settings are organized for successful learning and development (Nasir, 2000, 2002, 2005).

Two critical features of such community-based activities characterize successful learning settings for African American students. First, community-based activities where successful learning occurs are organized in ways that support students' sense of safety, belonging and identification, self-esteem, respect, and competence (Eccles and Gootman, 2002; Heath, 2004; Nasir et al., 2006). Second, these settings often incorporate important scaffolds that support the learning and performance of novices (Eccles and Gootman, 2002; Lave and Wenger, 1991; Nasir et al. 2006). These activities also offer specialized roles for youth (Heath, 2004; Nasir and Hand, 2008), are more likely to position youth as teachers and as learners, and are places where youth feel "at home" (Hirsch, 2005; Kim, 2004).

While these organizational features clearly influence learning outcomes directly since they support engagement and problem-solving, they also influence learning indirectly by offering participants access to identities as doers and learners of those practices. There is a growing body of literature on how individuals develop identities as they take part in activities (Boaler and Greeno, 2000; Holland et al., 1998; Wenger, 1998). I have described this process as the learning setting providing access to potential identity "resources" that individuals can take up or not as a part of their identities (Nasir, 2004; Nasir and Cooks, 2009).

In this chapter, I focus on these relations between processes of learning and processes of identity in learning settings outside of school, drawing on findings from several studies on identity and learning for African American students in high school basketball, high school track and field, and the game of dominoes. In some ways, this chapter serves as a comparison for the chapters about identities in school; while supporting identities is a key aspect of both in-school and out-of-school learning settings, the out-of-school settings that I studied were organized in ways that consistently fostered identities for participants as doers and learners.

Each of the three studies on which this chapter is based utilized a combination of observational and interview methods for studying students' learning and identity outside of school (see the Appendix for details of specific methods). All of these studies relied on close observations with small groups of students (usually around twenty) in order to capture the richness of their interactions in learning settings and to understand the nature of the learning settings themselves.

As we saw with Octavia, as some young people came to participate in and learn these practices, their identities as players were strengthened, which supported their future learning. Over time, then, identity and learning processes mutually supported one another as participation in these community activities became more sophisticated. Furthermore, young people's racialized identities (as African Americans) did not tend to conflict with learner identities in these learning settings. In other words, these practices were not racialized by society in ways that defined them as being out-of-scope for African American learners. In fact, these practices were racialized such that African American racialized identity was often viewed as being congruent with participation in these activities; this congruence was reflected in both the cultural history of these practices in the African American community and in the nature of talk among participants.[1] Young people, then, were not faced with conflicts between their cultural selves and their learner selves.[2]

The power of identity for students' engagement in and frame on learning is illustrated in the following comment by a high school basketball player, Vaughn, in answer to a question about why he plays the game:

> I play because it's fun. It's fun. It's fun. It's like, when I get angry, when I get frustrated, when I get sad, if I play basketball it kind of like leaves me, you know? And it's like basketball to me is like an art form, the

better I am in myself, the way I play describes who I am, you know. If it's dunking on somebody, going up strong and powerful, just aah! All in they face. So it's, I'm aggressive and I'm powerful and I'm really straightforward. But if it's sort of like a spin move, a finger roll, it shows finesse. It's like when I get to where I need to be, where I'm somewhat satisfied as a junior next year, you'd be able to watch me play basketball and know who I am.

Vaughn speaks to the relation between identity and learning in basketball for him. He articulates his strong sense of identity in the sport, aligning his sense of self with his way of participating in the sport and highlighting the way his basketball play is an expression of who he is. Importantly, Vaughn also conveys a sense of trajectory and the future learning that this strong identity will give rise to.

Vaughn captures, in a nutshell, one of the ways that learning and identity processes supported one another in learning practices outside of school for the African American students whom I studied. His comments highlight a perspective that views learning as being about gaining mastery in the domain of basketball. It is deeply linked to becoming more of who he wants to be and about finding and expressing himself through his play. From his perspective, learning in basketball does not require him to check his personality or his social self at the door.

I argue that in each of the out-of-school learning settings that I studied, this congruence between learning and identity processes is enabled by two key aspects of these practices: (1) the social organization of the practice and roles available within it, and (2) the opportunity of participants to personally contribute to the practice, to have something of themselves taken up and valued. Underlying both of these aspects of the practices were the ways that students' social and racial identities were viewed as being aligned with learning in these settings. These characteristics of out-of-school learning settings made them places where young people felt competent, found success, and saw themselves as belonging.[3] In the discussion that follows, I first illustrate the connection between learning and identity in the out-of-school practices that I studied; I then describe in more detail the two aspects of out-of-school practices that fostered this connection.

The Connection between Learning and Identity

It is a cold day in February. Dusk is beginning to threaten visibility, and the thirty-plus members of the high school track team are engaged in their usual routine. They are scattered about the track: the hurdlers on one part of the track, the sprinters on another, and the relay runners on yet another. The field events athletes are in the middle of the grass field on the inside of the track, and the jumpers are lined up near the sand pit. The athletes are all African American, about half girls and half boys. They conduct the business of their practice largely independently, with occasional prodding, feedback, or direct instruction from three African American coaches. The hard physical work being done by the student athletes is interspersed with chatting, teasing, and laughter.

Both identity work and learning happen routinely during the flow of activity here. Consider the following vignette. A group of female athletes are struggling to learn how to run hurdles; Octavia, introduced above, is among them. They are new to the sport and a bit anxious—in part because the hurdles make a loud crash when they are knocked over. Specifically, they are trying to learn how to take just three steps between each hurdle—or to three-step. Octavia takes off from the starting point. She clears the first hurdle and lets out a little squeal before clearing the second. The third hurdle falls to the ground with a crash, and Octavia, visibly frustrated, walks back toward the starting line. The coach, a thirty-something, stern-voiced African American man, has been watching, and the following conversation ensues:

Octavia: I can't get—
Coach: Look here kid.
Octavia: I can't—
Coach: Look here, you're gonna be a hurdler. That was the best that you've ever gone over any hurdle. That was the best that you've gone over any hurdle. Did you feel how much speed you had when you came off? But you have to control that speed when you get to the next hurdle, one two three up, out. [*He physically demonstrates for her.*]
Octavia: How many did I have, four?

Coach: Yeah . . . you had four, that's why it went over. [*Octavia walks back to the starting line area and gets in line.*]

This learning moment illustrates the ways that learning and identity occur together and are mutually supported in the practice of track. Clearly, this moment is instructional, in that much like a teacher, the coach evaluated Octavia's performance and offered her suggestions for improvement. However, just as she is given resources to improve her performance and learn to three-step, she is also given opportunities to develop a sense of identity as a hurdler.

Immediately after her attempt, Octavia evaluates her performance negatively, expressing frustration and the belief that she can't accomplish the task—she can't get over the hurdles. The coach responds with "look here, kid, you're gonna be a hurdler," which offers her an identity as a future hurdler—dismissing her negative assessment and encouraging a new perspective. He then reframes the performance: "That was the best that you've ever gone over any hurdle." In making this statement, he not only gives her a success, but he also shifts the criteria by which she might be evaluating her competence. He explains, "Did you feel how much speed you had?"—identifying the speed as a positive characteristic and pinpointing where improvement needs to occur—"but you have to control that speed when you get to the next hurdle." He follows this explanation with a physical demonstration of the appropriate movement.

Instructionally, the coach provides Octavia with information about how to more effectively run the hurdles and helps her to understand what progress and success are in learning to hurdle and how to recognize them. The learning happens as Octavia tries to improve authentic performance—prior learning is not seen as a prerequisite for engagement.

This is also an identity-building episode, with the coach repositioning Octavia as a competent participant and as a future expert. Her track identity may also be influenced by her becoming more skilled at running hurdles, as well as by her coming to evaluate performances and see the world through the disciplinary lens of an expert hurdler.

Octavia is learning to view her performance as an expert would, by understanding the multiple dimensions of the task of hurdling and evaluating herself by these dimensions, not simply by the outcome of the hurdle falling over. The coach explicitly tells her, "You're gonna be a hurdler," in part as a reassurance that she will learn the task and in part to frame her hard work as a component of a broader goal. In doing so, she is offered access to the framing of an expert.

In dominoes, teaching and learning were also a normative part of play. They occurred in the form of explicit feedback in moments of play, but also in the "postgame wrap-up" when players would spontaneously rehash important plays in the game and offer instruction to their teammates and opponents. As young people were learning to make more sophisticated plays, they were also becoming players—that is, taking on the identity of domino players. This included taking up the discourse style of the game and coming to view themselves as competent in the game.

The following is an example of learning and identity work in an exchange among teammates just after a domino game. (See the Appendix for a brief description of the game and its rules.) The scene takes place in the context of a high school domino tournament at an urban high school in Southern California. In the tournament as a whole, the players ranged quite a bit with respect to their prior experience with the game. Players were mostly African American males, with only a handful of female students participating. The tournament took place in a classroom at lunchtime, with several games running simultaneously. There were more observers than players, and the room had a festive atmosphere: students were talking, laughing, and eating snacks. Each game had a small crowd of observers commenting on the game and chatting. In the vignette, a winning team engages in a postgame wrap-up session in which they refer to specific plays in the game and revisit game decisions and play rationale. In doing so, these players support each others' learning, but they also reinforce their own and one another's identities as competent domino players. Interestingly, the players engage the researcher's video camera in this identity work. (Note that I paraphrase players' statements in brackets when they use potentially unfamiliar slang or specialized terminology.)

> [*Four male students have just completed a domino game. Tyler and Dupriest defeated Antwone and Joel. All players are still sitting at the table.*]
> Dupriest [*to Tyler*]: Ballgame was over a long time ago, I just wanted to keep playing 'cause I knew I was going to get the twenty-five.

[I could have won the game already, but I wanted to score twenty-five points first.]

[*He laughs. Both Joel and Antwone stand up and slowly walk away from the table.*]

Dupriest [*to camera*]: In America, that is called twenty-five. You know, big six and the big four, that's twenty. And the four and the ace, that would give me a quarter piece. So we'll see y'all next week. Monday—bright and early to whop on somebody else, you know. Thank you. Ty, you wanna say something, Ty?

Tyler: We outta here though. Thanks a million. [*They both look at the game board that remains on the table in front of them.*]

Dupriest: Look, cuz, look. [*He picks up a piece from the board.*]

Tyler: I seen it too, cuz. That's why I kept playing. I seen it coming.

Dupriest: It was five sixes out there and I had these two. So I wasn't fi'in to close myself up. [I knew that I had the two remaining sixes, so I wasn't going to lock the game.]

Tyler: When you played big six, I knew it was gonna be on them.

Dupriest: I seen his hand. [*Points to Joel's spot.*] I knew he had to play big four. When he showed me his hand, I knew he was gonna come.

In this postgame analysis, the two winning teammates engage in a boasting session with each other and to the camera. As they do so, they have a discussion of plays in the game with implications for understanding and communicating strategic game goals in those plays. Toward that end, Dupriest pushes for the importance of watching the board, saying, "It was five sixes out there," meaning that five of the total seven sixes were on the board. Dupriest also expresses that he was counting the dominoes. He recounts to his partner that he counted the five sixes on the board and the two he had in his hand and deduced that no one else had any fives. At that point he made a conscious decision not to lock the game and to keep play going and in doing so to continue to try to score. Dupriest's statement to the camera is also noteworthy. He explains a bit of domino terminology to the audience and says that they will be back next week to "whop on" somebody else. As in the track example, learning is supported through a discussion of important content, and identity is supported both indirectly through the development of a disciplinary lens and directly as the two boys boast about their skill and potential to win the next game (demonstrating their competence). Through the process of talking through the winning game, these players reinforce their identities as strong domino players and as future domino players.

Similarly, in basketball, players engage in frequent teaching and learning moments, both with peers and with coaches. Like dominoes and track, these learning moments serve the purpose of offering opportunities for the learning of content (dribbling skills, shooting skills, and defensive and offensive plays) and simultaneously of providing opportunity for the development of identity as a basketball player. This identity development occurs both through coming to learn the disciplinary lens of experts in the game and through being responsible for particular game outcomes and making unique contributions to the team.

I consider the relation between learning and identity in these out-of-school practices to be *congruent*; that is, processes of learning and processes of identity are aligned in the practice, such that they support one another. It is critical to note that congruence lies not simply in an internal sense of alignment on the part of youths, but rather in the messages they receive in the social context about whether or not they belong and are learners in the setting.

Across these practices, two characteristics stood out as supporting the congruence of learning and identity. First, both learning and identity were supported by the *social organization of the practice*, including consistent feedback and the availability of specific roles in which one is expected to become competent. That is, these practices were organized in ways that made competence available. Second, each of the practices offered young people the *opportunity to personally contribute* to the practice, to have something of themselves taken up and valued. This created a personal connection with the practice and supported identities in the practice. Additionally, in dominoes, track, and basketball, students did not encounter tension between their social and racialized identities and the learning activities that they engaged in as a part of these practices. In other words, who they were was accepted and affirmed as they learned and participated.[4] In the sections that follow, I describe these two characteristics of the practices in greater detail and illustrate them with moments of learning and identity construction from dominoes, track, and basketball.

Supporting Congruent Learning and Identities in Out-of-School Practices

The Social Organization of the Practice

The out-of-school practices that I studied were organized in ways that supported access to resources for learning and resources for developing a learning identity in the practice. This was fostered in part by norms in the practice concerning giving help readily, by the turn-taking structure, by the norms concerning playing with a partner, and by the public nature of play. These aspects of the social organization of domino play are illustrated in the next vignette, in which an elementary school player, David, is learning how to play. He is unable to independently complete a play, but the structure of the game (along with intense play-by-play feedback from his partner, Timothy) allows him to complete play successfully and thus supports both his learning and his potential emerging identity as a domino player.

> [*David initially takes the 4–1 from his hand and plays it on the 1–1 tile on the board. This is a plausible play, except that David violates the conventions of game play by playing the 4–1 with the 4 side against the 1 (the 1 side should be against the 1, so that there is a match). Timothy corrects him.*]
>
> Timothy: No, you can't do it like that! It's going that way now. [*He points to the 6–1. David moves the 4–1 over to the 6–1, trying to play the 4 on the 6.*]
>
> Timothy: No, man, no! You can't do it like that! [*Marco, his opponent, steps in to help by taking the 4–1 and moving it to the appropriate place on the 1–1. David takes the 4–1 and puts in back in his hand. He next takes the 2–3 from his hand and holds it out, looking at Timothy expectantly.*]
>
> Marco: No, no you can't play that!
>
> Timothy: Man, dumbo! Turn it around! [*Marco reaches out to turn the domino to the correct position.*]

David's learning and participation in the game is supported by game structures and norms. Specifically, the game is organized such that he is working with a partner (with points being earned jointly), which means that Timothy is highly invested in David making good plays. I note here that Timothy calling David "dumbo" might be taken as an unkind derogatory statement, but it also could be that David takes it as a part of the norm of teasing in the game. It might also be, however, that the name-calling detracts from the game feeling like a safe space in which David can make mistakes.

Another feature of the practice is that it is not unusual for players to help one another, and receiving support to make an appropriate play is an important resource for learning. The turn-taking structure of the game and its physical setup allows David to easily observe the play of others. This observation affords him the opportunity to notice patterns in the play of others over the course of several hands. As he is offered the support to learn how to navigate the strategic aspects of play, his identity as a domino player is strengthened. This comes into clear relief a few hands later in the game when David begins to take on the language of play and boasts about his playing ability.

Feedback   An important aspect of the structure of out-of-school practices is the availability of critical and supportive feedback offered in the moments of the activity. Such feedback makes learning an expected part of the practice and continually offers participants access to the next level of expertise. We see this in David's case; with feedback, David is offered a way to participate despite a low level of game knowledge, and thus he begins to move toward more competence. So one important feature of the game of dominoes is that its structure is flexible enough to allow for assistance during play.

Consistent, in-game feedback was also a part of the social organization of the practice of basketball. In the following scene, the team is practicing for an upcoming game that is an important game in their season, so practice is even more intense than usual. The following exchange occurs about forty-five minutes into the practice, and players are using one-half of the court to practice their defensive play, where they switch covering particular offensive players as the other team moves on the court. The team is divided into two squads for the purposes of this drill—some players are wearing white jerseys and playing offense, and the others are wearing red jerseys and playing defense. Both Vaughn and his teammates Kevin and

Samson are practicing the defensive play. As this vignette begins, players are on the court in their positions: one player from each scrimmage team is at the half-court line, and a player is preparing to bring the ball into play. The coach is standing between them and has just explained the "box" defense—a standard defensive play that involves each player guarding a certain portion of the court.

> [*The coach steps off to the side, and the offensive player brings the ball into play by stepping over the half-court line. The player with the ball (who is being guarded by Vaughn), passes it to his teammate right under the basket, after struggling a bit to find an open player to pass to. As the defensive players move and "swing," the coach verbally affirms that they are doing a good job. The player with the ball scores, and the coach gently chastises Vaughn for allowing this score.*]
>
> Coach: Aw, come on Vaughn, come on now. The guy you're guarding [in the upcoming game] is six inches taller. Come on. [*The other players laugh a bit and tease Vaughn briefly. The game continues as the ball goes back into play. This time the point guard dribbles to the right and passes again to the post player (just under the basket). Kevin is now guarding this player. He scores again.*]
>
> Coach: Uh-uh, OK now that time you gotta switch it, if he comes over the cross screen you bump below and switch, OK? On that cross screen. [*Players chat a bit and laugh. The point guard points to another player and says something teasingly. The ball goes back into play as the offensive player dribbles right, then back left, then passes to the middle. As Samson switches, Vaughn blocks the pass. The point guard claps to communicate to his team to pass the ball back to him, so he can refocus the flow of the ball.*]
>
> Coach: Alright, hold the ball on top, hold the ball on top. [*To a specific player*] Now especially when you got caught. OK, it was good that you switched, but you gotta yell "switch," cause what happened was you switched out which was a smart move, but Kevin came out too, because he didn't hear a "switch." So as soon as you know you are gonna switch, yell out "switch." [*To all players*] Whoever is the man that's switching out has got to call out "switch," then Kevin would know to take your man. [*Vaughn and the same other player as before*

are again jostling back and forth a little as the other player gets in posi-
tion to guard Vaughn and pushes against him a little. They both smile.]

Coach: OK, here we go, let's go box. [*The point guard dribbles left and*
then right at the top of the key. Kevin switches out.]

Coach: There you go Kevin! OK, good. Good good good. Call it out
loud, Sam, gotta say "switch." [*The ball goes to the player whom*
Vaughn is guarding on the right wing. Vaughn steps toward the player
with his arm up as the player shoots. The ball bounces off the rim.]

Coach: Box box box! [*Steve goes up and gets the rebound.*]

Coach: Alright, let's go up top. Now, chances are they're gonna knock
down our shots, so Vaughn, Vaughn, Vaughn make sure to close out
all the way on that shot, 'cause five times . . . at least half the time
they're gonna knock down that shot. [*The offensive player dribbles*
and another red player switches out to put his body between the player
with the ball and the basket.]

This vignette offers insight into the way feedback and thus access
to learning was made available to players. Players were learning a defense
whereby one blocks the other team from scoring. However, since this
competence depends on other smaller skills, such as attending to where
the ball is, dribbling, anticipating likely moves, and blocking shots by
jumping, the learning of those discrete skills was also being reinforced.

Early in the practice session, the coach provides detailed information about carrying out the defense in the context of the upcoming game
(in other words, he describes how the moves he is teaching would need
to be applied). This specificity about how to carry out the moves and who
has responsibility for carrying out which moves is consistent throughout
the interchanges. Also consistent is the explanation for when a particular
skill would be useful or important, such as when the coach tells Vaughn,
"Make sure to close out all the way on that shot, 'cause . . . at least half
the time they're gonna knock down that shot."

I should note that the defensive play that the boys were learning
to run is part of a standard set of defenses. This means, first, that players
are expected to learn and carry out these plays—they can't just go out on
the court and improvise. It also means, though, that they have access to
watching other players and teams carry out the same plays, and they have

the opportunity to learn from that observation. Thus, one aspect of the social organization of basketball is access to the modeling of important information.

Additionally, as in dominoes, feedback is consistently offered during practice. The coach gives instructions, the players try to physically carry out the play, and then they get immediate feedback. Players also provide feedback to one another, such as when the point guard claps to remind his team to return the ball to him. This feedback has two important purposes: correction and encouragement. For instance, early on, the coach expresses disappointment with Vaughn ("Aw, come on Vaughn, come on now"). But embedded in this statement of disappointment is also encouragement—carried in his tone, which implies, "I know you can do better than that." In this way Vaughn knows that his performance is not in line with the skill and potential the coach believes that he has. At the same time, the feedback offers specific and context-relevant ways for players to improve their practice.

Another form of feedback comes through the display and correction of mistakes. Mistakes in basketball are clear and public (for example, the point when the coach stops play to offer specific feedback to a player, such as telling Sam to call "switch"). However, mistakes are considered a normal part of the activity, and being corrected is not perceived as a challenge to one's ability. Multiple chances for players to try again are embedded in the practice, as well as playful teasing and joking about mistakes. With mistakes considered par for the course, making a mistake doesn't mean that one isn't a basketball player; it isn't in opposition to an identity of competence as a player.

Similarly, in the practice of high school track and field, feedback was a core component of the structure of the practice. For instance, in one practice, the coach watched a young woman run the 100-meter hurdles. When she finished, he gave specific and detailed feedback about the hurdling performance: "Oh great job! Great job! But you can't . . . the only thing I'm telling you, look up, is you can't . . . if you at any point start coming down here or you point your toe on the trail leg, that's the only reason why you'll hit them. You're low enough, you're attacking them now, and you're running between them, OK?" Sometimes feedback offered ways for the coach to tweak a runner's movement; at other times it was geared toward helping the runner perceive the environment in new ways. For example, the coach told a runner to listen to the rhythm of her footsteps as she ran: "You can hear and see it. . . . Good job. You should hear and see a distinct difference. [*He has her listen to the feet of another runner.*] It went from shu shu shu da da da. Did you hear the difference? OK." Such feedback supported novices in learning the movements of the sport but also in viewing practice and performers through the eyes of an expert—what Rose (2004) and Stevens and Hall (1998) have termed "disciplined perception."

Specific Roles   Another aspect of the out-of-school practices I studied that supports learning and identity is the fact that individuals in these practices are offered specific roles to carry out. These roles both delineate the knowledge and skills that students are responsible for learning and offer a specific form of expertise and identity within the practice.

In basketball, an obvious role is one's position on the team— whether one is a point guard, an off-guard, a center, or a forward. Players were assigned these specialized roles, which supported them in learning a particular subset of skills especially well. Importantly, these roles were also integral to the functioning of the team, and each role had a unique function that operated in the service of the team as a whole. This dynamic positioned the players as important assets to their team.

There are several times in the basketball vignette when the coach spoke to a player with a particular role and offered feedback to improve the play, along with a rationale for why that move or skill was important for a player playing that role. For instance, Vaughn played the off-guard position (between a guard and a forward), while Kevin played the center or the power forward position. Thus, Vaughn was responsible for strong defense and determining (to some degree) the flow of the ball during play, and Kevin was responsible for getting rebounds and scoring. These assigned roles were inextricably linked to each other through the practice, as illustrated when the coach told another player that calling out "switch" is the only way for players to decide their next moves.

Similarly, in track, student athletes were assigned (by the coaches) to compete in certain events. Possible roles in track include hurdler, jumper, relay runner, and sprinter. Importantly, although these roles were assigned, they were not assigned randomly; rather, they were made in line with the coaches' sense of the athletes' interests, skills, and potential. For instance, Octavia was identified as a potential hurdler by the coach, who then structured experiences and feedback for her to gain the skills a hurdler needs to know in order to perform well. As in the other practices, identity is supported indirectly by athletes increasing their skill at the role, by their developing the disciplinary lens supported by a particular role, by coaches fostering the development of relationships with other hurdlers, and by coaches providing direct verbal reinforcement (for example, "You're gonna be a hurdler").

In dominoes, the assignment to roles was much less explicit. Rather than be formally assigned specific roles, players took up and enacted roles as they played. In the following vignette, Timothy has clearly taken up the more expert/teacher role, while David (who is relatively new to the game and is learning the conventions of play) takes up the novice/student role.

> [*David hesitantly takes out a domino to make a play.*]
> Timothy: Call your money [points]. [*Timothy moves the domino to the proper spot on the game board.*]
> Timothy: Count, man look, count!
> David: Four, five . . . [*David points to the various ends on the board, unsure.*]
> Timothy: That's it! Call it!
> David: Five! [*Laughing.*]
> Timothy: Thank you! Finally got your money!
> David: Four, five . . . [*Counts again.*]
> Timothy: Finally, call your money. [*Two more plays pass.*] Alright, want some more money?
> David: Mo' money? No problem!

Timothy's role as expert allows him to offer support and feedback to David, and David, as novice, is allowed to receive help. Note that David also takes up the way that Timothy talks about play. For instance, the phrase, "Call your money" is repeated and becomes instantiated as a way to talk about scoring points. By this time in the game, David is clearly participating in this discourse, though his goals in play do not reflect the goal of scoring. David actually does score, though he does so accidentally. Also note the way in which Timothy, after David's accidental score, emphasizes the desirability of a scoring play with the question, "Alright, want some more money?" to which David answers, "Mo' money? No problem!" The language that David comes to use works to directly socialize him into the goals of scoring—despite his lack of knowledge about *how* to score (and indeed how to create a play independently). Here we see the beginnings of the process of a player developing competence and a sense of identity as David begins to speak the language of scoring.

This analysis has shown that both the social organization of these practices in general and the availability of specific roles within the practices worked to support novices as they learned to competently participate in the practices and as they came to see themselves as learners. Through structures and norms such as the availability of formative feedback, multiple opportunities for practicing a skill, and the expectation of growing competence in a specified role, young people in these practices could both gain skills and simultaneously see themselves as increasingly productive participants in the practice.

Personal Contribution and Social/Racial Belonging

Learning and identities in these practices were also afforded by the ways in which the practices gave youth the opportunity to personally contribute to the practice and to feel that their contributions were valued and taken up. We saw a bit of this in the discussion about roles; when participants have specialized roles, their contribution to the practice is unique, and often necessary for furthering the group goal, like winning a basketball game or a track meet.

In basketball, players put something of themselves into the practice as they took on the responsibility for decision-making in the context of the game. Players had the responsibility to make decisions by signaling their intention to others through their actions or by calling out plays. During game play this entailed split-second decision-making and drawing on ritual ways of communicating one's intentions to the other players. This occurs in a moment of basketball practice:

> Coach: Sam, you're gonna need to communicate, and if you see that
> he gets caught up, you're saying "switch" and you're stepping out in

> Bettencourt [the name of a player], so of course, if Sam's going to Bettencourt, he's gonna try to drive into Samson again so he gets it . . . and if there's a lull period, let's say they swing the ball around a little bit and Joseph, you and Samson and Bettencourt are on the other side, the weak side, you may have a chance to be able to switch, when they're dribblin' over here or whatever.

Competence is also about making good decisions about plays during the game and communicating those decisions to one's teammates. Here, the coach tells the players that it is their decision to determine when to call "switch"; and although the coach offers multiple possibilities for play, he leaves the final decision to the players—and this choice affects all of the other team members and the outcome of the play. The decision encompasses both talk and "stepping out" on Sam's part, which the other players would need to recognize in the repertoire of moves that Sam makes during games. Sam's decision to indicate a switch through his actions would cause a chain of events that would significantly change the course of everyone else's play. Thus, it is important for him to express it clearly and when he is sure that it is warranted.

This decision-making was part of a broader set of responsibilities that players shouldered. Players in basketball were accountable to one another for running the defense so that they could block shots of the opposing team or prevent them from scoring. They were also accountable for running the play, communicating, and paying attention to what the other team was doing, such that they could adapt the movements of the defense to what happened in the game. Thus, players were accountable for mastering a concrete set of skills and for making particular kinds of decisions in play.

Similarly, in track and dominoes, youth were responsible for carrying out particular responsibilities and made independent decisions as they did so. In track, runners were responsible for making their own decisions about using the starting blocks and about pacing themselves during their event. In dominoes, players alone decided which domino to play at each point in the game, when to score points, and when to offer assistance or feedback to other players.

Social Roles and Social Belonging   In basketball and track (and to a lesser degree in dominoes), in addition to formal roles with respect to players' responsibilities on the team, youth also had informal social roles that allowed them to contribute something of themselves to the practice above and beyond their skill in the sport. For instance, in track, nearly all of the athletes identified the social role they played on the team in addition to their formal positions. One athlete said that she was the "mama" of the team because she took care of everyone; another said he was the motivator and that he kept everyone "up" when things were not looking good during a meet. These roles not only gave youth a way to contribute personally to the team, but also fostered a sense of belonging and an affinity between their sense of personal identity and their participation in the sport. This sense of social belonging was fostered in other ways in track as well.

Because of the organizational structure of track practice and meets, there was quite a bit of downtime when the team was together. Meets were all-day affairs, with various events occurring throughout the day at different times. During meets, athletes and coaches spent the entire day together in the stands with a large cooler full of food and water; this created a lot of time for building relationships, sharing personal stories, and making connections.

The coach felt that having team members who were socially bonded and who trusted him made their performance stronger, and he created opportunities for this kind of social bonding to occur, including playing informal games of football with the athletes. As another example of the way that social belonging was purposefully fostered, during one practice the coach engaged four girls in a conversation about their future careers; then he took what they said and offered them a way to turn their respective careers into a collective business, weaving a picture of a future in which they were highly connected.

In this vignette, the coach is working with the girls' relay team. They are practicing smooth handoffs, which require them to pass the baton to one another as one runner finishes her leg of the race and another starts. The runners run at full speed repeatedly, so they are a bit tired. The coach passes time between runs by chatting with the girls (this also gives them a chance to catch their breath and rest for a moment).

He asks each of them what she wants to be when she grows up. He has asked Candice, who reports that she wants to be an obstetrician. Then he turns to the next girl:

Coach: Michelle what do you want to be when you grow up?

Michelle: A pediatrician.

Coach: A pediatrician? So we're gonna have a pediatrician and an obstetrician?

Michelle: Yep.

Coach: Maybe you guys could go into business together—Candice can deliver the babies and you could take care of them once they get here. OK. That's cool. Why do you want to be a pediatrician?

Michelle: 'Cause I have a way with kids.

Coach: You have a way with kids? Do you take care of them when they're sick? You give 'em, like, Tylenol? What's the grape stuff?

Michelle: With my little sisters, I used to—

Ella: —give the baby codeine. [*She laughs. The coach laughs too. There's more conversation about the medicine.*] What's your nickname? What's your nickname Michelle? [*There's more talk about nicknames. The coach plays around with nicknames for her.*]

Coach [*returning attention to the practice*]: You ready to do this one, Michelle?

Michelle: Yep.

Coach: Whenever you ready, Ell. [*Ella runs, but the timing is off and they miss the handoff.*]

Ella: I'm tired and I can't run no more!

Coach: That was right there.

Michelle: I got out that time.

Coach: Yeah, you got out two steps too early. One step too early and you'd be fine. Y'all were right on pace to get it right here. Right here Michelle would have had it in full stride. Let's try it again. [*Ella expresses frustration and walks back to her starting place.*] I know. I know. If you're that tired, then get it right. [*Returning to chat*] What you wanna be when you grow up Ella? [*She doesn't answer for a moment.*]

Ella: A hustler.

Coach: Did she say a hustler? . . . A hustler, no we don't want that, Ella.

Ella: Brett Favre. [This is a joke, as Brett Favre is a white professional football player.]

Coach [*pressing*]: Do you want to be a business person?

Ella: I want to be an entrepreneur.

Coach: What do you think you're good at selling?

In this interchange, the coach actively brings the athletes' social selves into the practice of their sport. While they are in the midst of practicing handoffs, he asks each athlete, in turn, what she wants to be when she grows up. As he elicits these responses, he engages in conversation with the team members that is largely social, suggesting a future in which three girls start a business together. The tone in this conversation is light and playful. All the while, the athletes are practicing a very difficult skill and are tired. This excerpt speaks to the ways both competence and belonging are fostered in the sport, supporting the athletes in strengthening their identities as learners in track. The exchange conveyed to athletes that their social selves were accepted and valued in the context of their sport.

Identities as track athletes were also supported through the creation of a sense of belonging to a national track community. Former team members who had gone on to college regularly returned to attend practices, and the coaches and athletes discussed other athletes whom students would compete against in meets and those in the national rankings. On one trip the coach opened a national track magazine in a bookstore with the athletes and talked about the kinds of results one needs to rank nationally and shared the names of local athletes in the magazine. He pointed out, in particular, athletes from the same school district or young people the students might know. In doing so, he conveyed that "people like you" are successful at track, thus confirming the possibility of a future contribution to the sport.

Social belonging was also encouraged in dominoes. The structure of the game and the norms around social interaction within it sent a clear message to players about the space for their contributions being valued and taken up and the social identities that were accepted as a part of game play. Often, this bringing of self to the practice occurred in the form of humor and the use of African American language practices. Norms around these practices created opportunities for players to demonstrate linguistic wit, humor, and skill in the game. In the following vignette from an adult domino game, Willie uses metaphorical language, nuance, and African American Vernacular English (AAVE) in an illustration of how the practice of dominoes incorporates the social lives of the players. The game board is shown below.

> [*The domino is on Willie, and it is his partner Ricky's play. Willie's last play was the 4–1.*]
>
> Willie: What you talkin' about? My partner fi'in to set me loose. [What do you mean? My partner's going to make a play that will allow me to domino.]
>
> Ricky: Want me to set you free? [*The tone here is silly and boastful, but he seems to understand Willie's request.*]

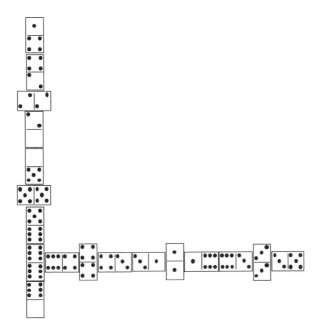

The game board after Willie's play.

Willie: Free like a bird, partner. I'm'a sing that song. 'Cause I know
   you! . . . I ain't got but one domino! The way my partner play. . . .
   Why you think I put that out there? [*Willie is speaking to Ricky,*
   telling him to pay attention to his last play as a hint as to what he has
   left in his hand. Ricky plays the 0–1 on the 1–4 to score five points.]
Ricky: Nickel.
Willie: My partner's drunker than a skunk. [*The group laughs.*]
Willie [*to Ricky*]: Whyn't you set me free? The domino ain't on you!
   [Why didn't you play a tile that I could play on?]
Ricky: Hey, I'm gone, man. [I'm going to domino myself.]
Observer: See what happens when people get greedy.
Willie [*to Ricky*]: No, the domino on me! [I was scheduled to domino
   this hand.]
Ricky: You got ace or what?

Willie uses the metaphor of a bird to impress upon his partner how
important it is that he play so as to permit Willie to keep the domino
(that is, to be the first to run out of tiles). He points to his last play as
being particularly relevant—essentially telling him not to play on that
end. One purpose of this talk is clearly instruction: Willie is trying to
encourage Ricky to make a certain kind of play. But the playful stylized
language also serves its own function—to liven up play and to make the
game an expressive endeavor. When Ricky ignores Willie's instruction,
Willie laughs and jokes "my partner's drunker than a skunk." Willie's
personality and language enrich and become a part of the play itself,
fostering a sense of belonging.

As with track, the players took up social roles with one another.
In adult play the older men often acted as guides for the younger men,
both with respect to strategic expertise in the game, but also in relation
to life concerns outside of the game. In one instance, one of the younger
men in the group had received a phone call from a woman who was
not his wife. One of the older men answered the phone and (knowing
it was not the other man's wife) asked, "Is this his wife?" During the
domino game the next day, the older man brought up this incident and
jokingly conveyed that anytime a woman called that was not a man's
wife, he would ask that question, in part to reinforce that a married man

shouldn't engage in any inappropriate conversations with a woman who is not his wife. In this exchange, the older man is taking up a role as an older advisor to the younger player.

As another example of social roles and social belonging, the next vignette depicts an interaction that both suggests belonging through the use of AAVE forms and humor and illustrates how dominoes can become a forum for discussions around important social issues. A player capitalizes on multiple potential meanings of the word "heavy" both to comment on the quality of play and to provide a social commentary on the current clothing trends of the younger generation. Willie is an older member of the group, in his early fifties, and Ricky is one of the group's youngest members, in his early twenties. Ricky wears his pants in a style characteristic of his age group, hanging low on his hips (called sagging). This style is in marked contrast to that of the older members of the group, whose appearance is more traditional and conservative. Doug, also involved in this interaction, is a game spectator and is waiting for his turn to play. The game is close in terms of points, and Doug is speculating on the potential game outcomes:

> Doug [*to Willie*]: Y'all might win, but I think Ricky might be getting a little heavy over there.
> Willie: That's OK, I'll carry him. Long as he don't have rocks in his pockets!
> Doug: I think he got a pocket full of rocks!
> Willie: That's why his pants won't stay up! [*Laughter around the table.*]

Doug initially uses the word "heavy" to comment on Ricky's play, implying that Ricky may not be carrying his own weight in the game (that is, not scoring any points for his team). Willie responds to Doug by saying that he could "carry" Ricky (or score a sufficient number of points for his team), as long as Ricky is not too heavy (that is, "have rocks in his pockets"). A moment later, Willie returns to the metaphor of the rocks in his pockets to comment on the style of sagging pants that Ricky (and his generation) wears. Willie signifies by playing on the game-specific use of the term "heavy," elaborating it, and then reinterpreting it in a literal way to tease Ricky about the new style of pants. Here, "heavy" becomes a metaphor for struggling for points; "carry him" becomes a metaphor for picking up the slack in the points; "rocks" becomes a metaphor for useless dominoes. Doug's initial comment about Ricky being heavy is also important. It serves to critique Ricky's play and perhaps attune him to the game goal of scoring, in that the public teasing about being heavy or not scoring enough points could serve to communicate to Ricky that the goal of scoring is important at this point in the game.

This is another example of the way talk in dominoes served a teaching function with respect to strategy, and it illustrates how Willie used sophisticated double meanings to chide the younger player about a clothing style he viewed as inappropriate. Dominoes thus was not only a place where players could express personal opinions and talk about social matters, it was also a place for a kind of mentoring with respect to manhood (such as when the older man answered the phone and took on the role of advisor to the younger man).

Social belonging was also a key aspect of the practice of basketball. The basketball coach described each player as having key social roles in addition to their formal positions on the team. The following two comments from basketball players Edward and Carter articulate the social roles they perceive themselves to have on the team:

> Edward: Yeah. . . . Because I feel like I bring to the team or whatever, like leadership, and I just try to help people when they need help. And like this year, the big change was I became more of a factor, than like last year he [the coach] was using me for defense and then this year it was offense.

> Carter: I defend the other team's best player. And then offense, getting the plays started, getting us into the offense, and just being a leader out there—you know they see me going at it and playing hard then they usually just follow my example. I'm not a real talkative leader, I just show by example. So if they see me pushing myself, then they push themselves.

Through these social roles the players express themselves, inserting their personalities and emotions into the roles to make the established positions their own. Edward identifies his social role as bringing leadership to the team and helping others when they need it. This role is important in that leadership and support for other players in difficult game moments can make the difference between winning and losing. Carter's social role is similarly critical to the success of the team. He expresses his enthusiasm for the sport as he carries out his position, "getting the plays started, getting [the players] into the offense, and just being a leader out there."

Thus, these social roles were avenues for self-expression, as well as important aspects of these players' success in fulfilling their basketball positions on the team. However, I should note that these roles are different in nature from the kinds of social roles that I described in the other practices. These are not general social roles, but rather social roles in relation to the practice of basketball. Nonetheless, they incorporated aspects of players' personalities. Players felt as though they occupied a unique and valued place on the team by virtue of these roles.

In addition to the social roles players took on, players had opportunities to feel like they could "be themselves" in basketball. Practices were characterized by a significant amount of teasing and laughter, which was an accepted part of the practice and offered players a chance to "be who they are" and have fun. In the basketball vignette above, despite the fact that players are doing serious work, there is lightness around the work, particularly in the small moments of interaction between the plays. Note that the coach does not prohibit these arguably "off-task" interactions; they are not viewed as a problem for players completing the work of basketball practice.

Thus far, I have focused primarily on the ways that social belonging and self-expression were fostered in track and field, dominoes, and basketball. These examples also illustrate that these practices were not racialized in ways that indicated the exclusion of African American participants. Being African American was not considered a problem for full participation in any of these practices. This was likely due to both the fact that these were almost entirely African American spaces and the fact that being African American was not viewed as being evidence that one could not succeed in them. But even beyond the phenotype of the participants, African American language and cultural practices were part and parcel of these learning spaces. For instance, in the examples presented, young people often used AAVE in their communication with one another and with coaches. Additionally, there were no negative stereotypes about the ability of African American youths to play dominoes, play basketball, or run track. This lack of negative stereotypes meant that their competence was not at stake by virtue of their race.

Furthermore, in all of these practices there were moments when discussions of race and African American identity came up explicitly. In track, this occurred both when the team was running against largely white teams and when the coach cautioned athletes not to be intimidated by athletes from whiter, wealthier teams. During one meet, held at a college campus, the track coach explicitly taught the students how to say "good morning" to every person they passed on campus (almost all of whom were white). In other words, the coach was engaged in an active racial socialization of the athletes, with respect to both how to interact with white people and how to think about being African American. In basketball, the high school coach encouraged the players to be "scholar-athletes" and warned them that less would be expected of them because of their race—that is, the majority would not expect them to be students—and that they must shoulder these negative stereotypes and create positive identities. Again, explicit racial socialization occurred here.

Conclusion

The experiences and interactions described here highlight several important points about the nature and process of learning and identity in practices outside of school for these African American students. First, learning and identity processes mutually supported one another in moments of activity—both were made available to participants in multiple ways. Specifically, learning and identities in these practices were supported by the social organization of play, including the presence of clear roles; opportunities for having something of oneself valued and taken up; and the assumption that participants' racialized identities, as African American, did not conflict with the dispositions and skills required of players and participants.

The presence of these supporting processes is both remarkable and quite ordinary. It is remarkable that these factors mirror what we know about positive learning spaces in school, and yet learning settings with these properties are rarely seen in public schools attended by the majority of our nation's African American students. It is quite ordinary in that these learning settings were *routinely* structured in the ways that we have described—the social organization of play, the opportunity for having something of oneself taken up, and the congruence of racialized and learning identities occurring regularly in these practices and thus not being considered remarkable.

I reported this data on out-of-school learning settings first in part to seed an implicit counterexample to how learning and identity processes unfold in many public school settings. Chapter 3 considers the ways that African American students make sense of what it means to be African American, particularly in relation to stereotypes about African Americans common in our society and in their schools.

Notes

Portions of this chapter are adapted from N. Nasir and J. Cooks, "Becoming a hurdler: How learning settings afford identities," *Anthropology and Education Quarterly* 40:1 (2009): 41–61, used with permission from the American Anthropological Association; N. Nasir and V. Hand, "From the court to the classroom: Opportunities for engagement, learning, and identity in basketball and classroom mathematics," *Journal of the Learning Sciences* 17:2 (2008): 143–161, used with permission from Taylor and Francis Group; and N. S. Nasir, "Everyday pedagogy: Lessons from track, basketball, and dominoes," *Phi Delta Kappan Magazine* (March 2008), used with permission from the Phi Delta Kappan International.

1. As I discuss later in this chapter, although these particular practices did not support conflicts between the sense participants had of themselves racially and as learners, this does not mean that these practices were devoid of issues of power or privilege. Indeed, in basketball and dominoes, the available identities were quite gendered, such that learning identities in these practices may have been less available to female participants. This raises the issue that no cultural practice is neutral.

2. However, it should be noted that although the ways that these practices were racialized did not pose contradictions for the African American participants whom I studied, they might well have been gendered in ways that female participants did find problematic. I do not intend to imply that because they took place outside of school, the practices described in this chapter were "unproblematic" for students' identities.

3. Belonging, thus, can be conceptualized as a precursor to identity—when one feels like one belongs in a social or learning setting that then supports the development of one's identity as a learner in that setting.

4. The congruence I describe is a property of the practices that I studied and their location in predominantly African American schools and communities. I do not mean to imply that all out-of-school practices will have this congruent property, nor that these practices, in other places or during other historical times, would. Indeed, the inclusion of African Americans in professional sports is relatively new in U.S. history.

3

Wrestling with Stereotypes

Some people stereotype African Americans as drug dealers, gang bangers, and people that don't do nothing with their life.

—Clem, African American high school student

I think [stereotypes about African American students] just has been instilled in the American mind frame, like people just automatically categorize you and like, even people that don't try or don't really want to categorize you, 'cause I find it in myself, even though I don't want to categorize someone, but there are certain stereotypes that pop in your head and you have to catch yourself and say, no, that's not true. But it's gonna take a lot. And just like, I see that, people really believe those stereotypes or make judgments based on those stereotypes.

—Jordan, African American high school student

CLEM AND JORDAN DESCRIBE the ways that stereotypes about African Americans seem to operate automatically and consequently go virtually unexamined in American society. Clem offers a definition of the content of common stereotypes about African Americans, and Jordan notes the difficulty in changing these stereotypes, both because they are pervasive and because many people believe them. In Chapter 2, I alluded to the nature of the stereotypes about African Americans as belief systems that often can be found "hanging in the air" in learning settings inside and outside of school. In this chapter, I focus specifically on the in-school context as one where stereotypes not only hang in the air but also play out for students. I highlight student perspectives about stereotypes of African Americans and reflect on the role these stereotypes play in conversations among African American students about what it means to be black.

The questions of how society views African Americans and the role of perceptions about race in preventing access to institutions and resources are longstanding themes in the works of African American scholars. In 1903, African American researcher W. E. B. Du Bois directed a poignant question to African Americans: "What does it feel like to be a problem?" With this question, Du Bois captured the essence and dilemma of black life in the United States—how does one psychologically process the framing of one's community and one's existence as problematic, while simultaneously seeking to achieve educationally? One way that ideas about African Americans as "problems" have been maintained and perpetuated has been through stereotypes.

Drake (1987) argues that color prejudice and racism, in the form of assumptions about the character and capacity of African Americans, have long been prevalent in the United States. He quotes Thomas Jefferson, who said in 1793: "This unfortunate difference of colour, and perhaps of faculty, is a powerful obstacle to the emancipation of these people. . . . I advance it therefore, as a suspicion only, that the blacks, whether originally a distinct race, or made distinct by time and circumstances, are inferior to the whites in the endowments both of body and mind" (14). Jefferson questions the "faculties" of African Americans and "suspects" that blacks are inferior to whites in both body and mind. Drake argues that representations of African Americans as inferior and stereotypes of blacks as being less intellectually capable are deeply rooted in American thought and culture. Research has identified several main stereotypes about African Americans, and the literature is quite cohesive on these: that blacks have low intelligence, engage in antisocial behavior, and lack an achievement orientation (Devine and Elliott, 1995; Hudley and Graham, 2001; Krueger, 1996).

The pervasive presence of stereotypes and prejudice in American society was initially tied to desires to maintain a system of free labor (slavery) while justifying the subhuman treatment of Africans and African Americans (Frederickson, 2002). Sociologist Larry Bobo (1999, 2001) argues that stereotypes are distinct social forces and thus part of a broader relative positioning between social groups in society. He contends that since stereotypes connect to a broader system of subjugation, they act to maintain inequality between racial/ethnic groups.

But what role do stereotypes play in the lives of contemporary youths as they make sense of what it means to be African American? Are stereotypes still alive in this "postracial" era? In this chapter, I present data from a study of racial identity, stereotypes, and math learning and achievement for African American students in a diverse northern California high school. My colleagues—Michael Davis, Kathleen O'Connor, and Grace Atukpawu—and I sought to understand the ways that race played out in math classrooms for African American students and the ways that racial identity was shaped and expressed within school and classroom life. The study involved multiple methods, including both qualitative and quantitative components. We surveyed more than five hundred students, conducted interviews with seventy students (more than fifty of whom were African American), and conducted hundreds of hours of classroom observations. I draw primarily on thirty-six interviews with African American students (conducted in the second and third years of the study). I draw on these data in particular to better understand how, in their own words, African American students think about race, when and how it is important to their lives at school, and how stereotypes play out in that sense-making process. I begin by describing the school context in greater detail.

School Context

This research took place at what I will call Washington High School, an ethnically diverse school in a suburb of a large city in California, with a student body of more than fifteen hundred. The demographics were as follows: 38 percent Hispanic, 23 percent black, 20 percent white, 18 percent Asian and Pacific Islander, and 1 percent Native American. Thirty-one percent of students qualified for free or reduced-price lunch, 25 percent were designated as English Language Learners (ELL), and

23 percent had parents who were college graduates. Students and teachers alike took great pride in the diversity of the school and viewed it as a unique positive characteristic of their experience at Washington. Many of the classrooms displayed posters with antiracism messages, and both teachers and administrators shared the value of accepting and valuing cultural differences. In our interviews with twenty-four students (from both genders and a range of racial groups) in the first year of our study, almost all of them used the word "diverse" to describe the school when asked, "Tell me about your school." For instance, one student responded: "This school is diverse. There's a lot of different people at this school. You'll never see just one race kicking it with each other—it's all together. It don't matter what color you are—it's like a unit—it's like family almost."

Although diversity was highly valued at the school, there were patterned racial differences in the courses students took and in their achievement in mathematics. Teachers, who had conducted an analysis of their students' grades and test scores, reported these differences to us, and we later verified these patterns through our own examination of achievement and course-taking data. Similar to Pollock's (2005) findings, race at Washington was not often talked about in public spaces, but it was often noticed as a category that was used to explain and understand achievement outcomes.

The aim of this chapter is to better understand the ways that African American students were thinking and talking about race at Washington and to examine the role that stereotypes played in students' sense-making about race.

Racial Stereotypes in Math Class: "Y'all Too Black"

The issue of stereotypes was not one that we sought to study at Washington, but it seemed to be staring us in the face as we observed mathematics classrooms and interviewed students. For instance, the following interactions from an algebra classroom illustrate how African American students sometimes talked about race.[1]

During a group activity in which students were solving problems together, an African American female, Catherine, asked her African American male peer, "Why you eatin' that Snickers bar like a slave? . . . You know how slaves used to have to eat out of their hands and stuff." Other students laughed. Subsequently, Catherine needed help with the math, so she (on behalf of the group) solicited help from the (substitute) teacher. The teacher encouraged the group to discuss the math problem among themselves; however, the group instead chatted socially. A few moments later, the teacher reprimanded the group for not working, and they accused her of not helping when they asked for help. The students then reengaged in a discussion about math. Shortly after, Catherine began to sing, and when her peer asked why she was singing, she responded, "Because I'm black." A few moments later she chastised her classmates using similar language: "Ya'll too black . . . [you're] uncivilized."

I open with this example from classroom discourse because it illustrates that racial stereotypes were alive and well in this high school mathematics classroom and that they found voice among African American students. What comes to the surface in this exchange is a set of implicit understandings, an underground narrative, about race that students spoke of in interviews. It is particularly interesting that Catherine made references to race three times in this exchange—the first, about slavery (likening the eating habits of her classmate to that of a slave); the second, offering her own blackness as an explanation for why she sang in class; and the third, when she argued that some of the other African American students were "too black" and thus "uncivilized."

These characterizations of blackness and what it means to be African American align with societally shared stereotypes about African American people and often outright racist notions of what constitutes "black" behavior (for example, being uncivilized is equivalent to being "too black"). In other words, students are wrestling with these stereotypical notions about African Americans. The invocation of these themes in this episode signal that some students at Washington were struggling with their meaning and relevance—and indeed this was confirmed in interviews.

What It Means to Be African American

How did African American high school students at Washington think about what it means to be African American, both generally and in relation to school and mathematics? Our research team gained insight into this question when we organized focus groups with African American students at the school and asked them simply, "What does it mean to be black?" The consistency of students' answers to this question at Washington, and then at two other schools where we organized similar groups, was surprising. Most often students at Washington offered answers such as having a negative attitude toward school, listening to hip-hop music, being gangsters, or wearing the latest clothing styles. Occasionally, students mentioned what might be considered more positive characteristics, such as understanding African American history or doing well in school.

While certainly there were nuances with respect to how students interpreted these characteristics in relation to themselves and their communities, the consistency in the reports of students was striking. How might we interpret such responses? They should not be interpreted as an indication of "maladaptive" or ill-formed identities on the part of young people as individuals. Rather, these responses indicate that a powerful ideological force exists that keeps these stereotypes salient in the minds of us all. Jordan's comment at the opening of this chapter illustrates this point. He remarked that the stereotypes about black males (a demographic group to which he belongs) are so strong that he had to actively work to remind himself that they lacked truth. In the following section, I explore how African American high school students thought about what it means to be African American and how stereotypes were implicated in these definitions.

In our interviews with African American students, four themes emerged. First, many students felt that the racial categories of African American or black *did not capture the nuances* and complexities of their racial and ethnic identities, yet they knew that there was no space within our society to articulate and hold these more complex identities. Second, students overwhelmingly identified the *prevalence of stereotypes* and *having to manage stereotypes that others held* about African Americans as salient aspects of the experience of being African American. Third, students identified the *history of collective struggle and facing inequality* as important aspects of being African American. Fourth, students by and large held these conceptions of what it meant to be African American along with a conflicting set of ideas that *race did not matter* or lacked direct connection to their experience in the world or in the school.

Not Capturing the Nuances:
Labels That Essentialize

For many of the students whom we interviewed the label "African American" or "black" felt too limiting and did not capture the fullness and complexity of their ethnic heritage. Although all students indicated that "African American" and "black" were the closest match for them when they were filling out forms that asked for ethnicity, 31 percent of them said that their racial identity was more complex than these labels suggest. Jackie, for instance, said that she would check the "African American" box if she had to declare her racial group on a form, but, she added, "Also Creole, 'cause my dad is Creole and my mom is Jamaican." Similarly, LaToya said: "I'm an African descendant but American. I'm Cherokee too. But I don't put that down." In response to the question "What makes African Americans unique?" Lettie said, "'Cause they come from the same ancestry. There are so many different kinds of African American."

Both Jackie and LaToya articulate the complexity of their racial heritage and argue that when they check the African American box, they leave out important aspects of who they are. Lettie points out that although African American people share a particular ancestry, there are "so many different kinds" of African Americans; in other words, it's difficult to come up with just one definition about what it means to be African American.

Joeseph made a similar point and also highlighted another challenge with conforming to the racial boxes: "I'm mixed with black, French, Chinese, Haitian, Indian. But I check African American because that's what I've been around, but I don't really like to do that. 'Cause you become a part of the statistics. Like, uh, like AIDS—black women have more chance of catching AIDS—and black men are in jails. That's why I don't like doing that. I would like to check different ones." Joeseph argues that once people acknowledge they are African American, they "become a part of the statistics." In other words, they are seen negatively as members of a group that is *defined* by negative statistics, such as the high rates of having AIDS and being in jail. In Joeseph's case, he would like to have a box to check that carries less burden with respect to how others view the group.

Thus, a major theme in our conversations with young people about their African American identity was the complexity of defining racial and ethnic heritage. Students felt that their racial and ethnic heritages should not have to be reduced to oversimplified labels. Although they articulated their frustrations with the use of labels, students also didn't feel as though they had a choice. In short, many students felt ill represented by the choice of racial labels. This finding points to students' sense that the essentialized nature of racial labels was both ill fitting and overly constraining and didn't capture the fullness of students' identities.

The Prevalence of Stereotypes

In our interviews with young people, they routinely highlighted the significance of negative stereotypes in the racialized social terrain that they navigated in school and elsewhere in their lives. Sixty-four percent of them mentioned the negative stereotypes others have of African Americans as a part of their answer to the question, "What does it mean to be black?" Several specific stereotypes emerged repeatedly in students' descriptions. At the opening of this chapter, Clem noted the stereotypes of "drug dealers, gang bangers" and "people that don't do nothing with their life." Anthony echoed this view, saying "you got your stereotypes—he's a gangsta, he's a thug." Joeseph said: "White people dislike [having] black people around. I get looked at like a threat wherever I go. . . . It's stereotypes. You get looked at different than other people. When I walk down the street in [this city], I just came from an SAT prep program, trying to get myself ready, when I walked down the street everyone was looking at me like you don't belong here." And Brian said: "A lot of people fear the fact that I'm a black man and I wear the clothes that I do and I act the way that I act. But if they actually sat down and got to know me, they would know that I'm not a threat at all, and a lot of the times—a lot of people—you should never judge a book by its cover."

These students all point to the prevalence of the stereotype of African Americans as potential threats—as thugs or potential criminals. Young men in particular were not only highly aware of the existence of this stereotype, they felt that the stereotype was often applied especially to *them*, and they experienced this application of the stereotype as conveying the message that they don't belong and are to be feared.

Other students set their discussion of stereotypes within a broader context of societal inequality. In other words, stereotypes did not exist just in the heads of others but were part of a broader system of privilege and marginalization. For example, Arthur talked about facing discrimination from the police and from store clerks and argued that other students respond to him as though he *were* a stereotype at school. He pointed to both his race and his size as important factors in the kind of discrimination he faced and connected this struggle to an historical chain of acts of oppression:

> Arthur: Like, black people, it's like, I don't know, you came from like, most came from Africa. We came over here on a boat by the white man, and then went through slavery, and then had fights like the Civil War, we won. And then yeah.
>
> Interviewer: OK.
>
> Arthur: And talking about like stuff we go through today.
>
> Interviewer: What do you think black folks go through today?
>
> Arthur: Like, what I go through is like when I was in east Oakland in the '90s. If I was by myself and the police pull me over for no reason, after a subject or somebody. And I'm like "what they do?" Basically just messing with me or whatever. Or like when I go to stores, I get followed around by the store [clerk] or whatever, getting looked at. I don't like that either.
>
> Interviewer: Does any of that stuff happen? What does it mean to be black at this school?
>
> Arthur: Like, I don't know. It's like, I guess it's intimidating when I walk down the hallway, people move out of my way and stuff. And like I don't know. I remember this one time, there was this one lady, she was holding her purse real tight, I can't take it anyway, like a little old lady, why would I take it from an old lady? She was like "I can't take you."
>
> Interviewer: OK. Anything else that you would say? So people are afraid of you because you're black.
>
> Arthur: Not just 'cause I'm black; I'm big too. But black is a part of it.

Interviewer: OK.

Arthur: I feel like, my cousin got pulled over too. Like 'cause he gots a grill [gold teeth], cops pulled him over 'cause his dreads [dreadlocks]. They pulled him over with like four cop cars, he was coming from night school. And he lived in [the city], so it was a white area, so I guess that's why they messed with him.

Arthur describes the kinds of discrimination that he routinely faces in the world, as others make assumptions about him because of his size and race. At the root of his experiences are the stereotypes others hold about African American males and the types of interactions that ensue when people enact their belief in those stereotypes. Arthur describes such experiences both inside and outside of school: fellow students "move out of [his] way" in the hallways, and an elderly woman appears to think he is going to steal her purse.

Similarly, Geoffrey drew on his own life experiences as evidence of how people act on their stereotypes about African Americans:

Geoffrey: Like, Devante, the thing about Devante you know, he's kind of, just by looking at him, you look at his dreadlocks you think "Oh he's probably going to act real ghetto, dress ghetto, talk ghetto," like with a total grill [gold teeth], but he has a 3.6 or 3.7 grade point average. But people don't notice that, you know what I mean? So like, basically . . . they think that being black you're suppose to not move on to college and do something. Or the only way you're suppose to go to college. I had surgery in the hospital and I remember I was just sitting there waiting and I remember the nurse came in, and she's all "Oh what college are you going to?" At that time I hadn't even decided. "What do you want to major in?" "Biochemistry." "Oh you want to be a doctor too?" And I'm like, "Not necessarily, 'cause I don't know how it would be to be a doctor." She's like "Why don't you just go to trade school or something?" Me'n my mom started looking at her funny like, trade school! Like you know what I mean? And she's like, uh, "Go to Heald College" [a business college] . . . She's like "Uh, why don't you do something like that? You can go to a nursing program, you don't have to go to school for so long." And she just started saying a whole bunch of bullshit. . . . at first I was thinking "Is she saying that 'cause I'm black or something?" I was in dreads and baggy clothes, so she probably didn't think I was intelligent—she had no idea. So, you know what I mean?—I don't know.

Geoffrey offers two examples of the ways that the assumptions of others about African Americans can be misleading with respect to education. First, he describes his friend Devante, who is a good student despite assumptions that he isn't because of his race and the way he dresses and looks "real ghetto." Second, he describes an incident when a nurse discouraged him from becoming a doctor and suggested that he aim for trade school instead.

Other students talked about the stereotypes at school that marked who was smart and academically successful. For instance, Jacob argued that there are stereotypes about who can be smart in math:

> Interviewer: Do you think race matters at all? How people experience school?
>
> Jacob: Uh, naw. It shouldn't. It don't. No it shouldn't matter. Because a lot of people will, I don't know. A lot of people will, um, stereotype—like people think, you know, if you're Asian you know a lot about math, and you like a math expert. And just because you're Asian doesn't mean that you know everything. It could be like somebody who's Mexican [knows] just as much. You know. Just as much. It's not really like that, it's like everybody, I don't know. It's not really like that, it's not racist at all. Race doesn't matter.

Jacob challenges the perspective which he has heard others express that puts forth the claim that only Asians can be good at math. He then argues that race doesn't matter. For Jacob, stereotypes about race play out in the form of the low expectations others hold for academic achievement. In particular, he views the stereotype that Asians are good at math as also being a negative stereotype of other, non-Asian students, perhaps because this stereotype is inherently comparative.

Several students articulated that either they or others held stereotypes that African American students were not as smart as other students. Jasper noted, "Well most people [think] we're loud, we're not educated, we're just ignorant, which is not true." But Joeseph said, "I don't think black students are doing as well as the other students." And Martin said, "I used to think that white people were smarter than black people. But like when I got here this year, I thought it wasn't true." These students make the point that African American students are often viewed as being less smart, less good at school, and less intellectually capable. Some struggled with these stereotypes themselves. And Martin indicates that he revised the stereotype he held about black students not being as smart as white students, an example of how students' continued interactions in the world can be cause for them to rethink stereotypes and choose alternative narratives about race.

As these student comments highlight, stereotypes are central in students' experiences generally and of being black in particular. Stereotypes, then, act as a racialized narrative that defines students' interactions with others to some degree. And in some cases, stereotypes cause others to fear black students or consider them as less capable in school. In school and elsewhere young people reported facing discrimination or poor treatment that was based on stereotypes about African Americans. Furthermore, African American students sometimes endorsed these stereotypes, linking them with broader social patterns and the history of oppression of African Americans in the United States. This highlights students' awareness of the social and historical context of these racialized narratives.

Black as Being "Ghetto"   Like Geoffrey, students sometimes invoked the term "ghetto" to refer to a particular version of blackness. For these students, ghetto epitomizes people who are loud, rowdy, speak slang, and don't abide by the same social rules as others. In answer to the question "How would you describe being black?" Brittany said simply, "Oh . . . some people stereotype like loud, ghetto." Marshall expressed the same sentiment: "'Cause most people [think] if you black you gotta act ghetto and speak slang."

Similarly, Whitney explained how she invokes this idea about blackness as ghetto when she "plays around" with her little sister, but also sees it as a stereotype that others have of African Americans: "Because people label being black as being ghetto, and if you're black you want to fit in with other black people so you can get to be ghetto. But like I'll say to my little sister, blood, you're hecka loud—I can't stand black people, just playing around like that, and oh, I can tell you're black." Later, Whitney used ghetto to describe how she was categorized by a white person: "That's what peoples say, they're like, like a white person said to me, 'You're not ghetto like I expected.' I'm like why do I have to be ghetto? . . . It's a stereotype that all black people are ghetto."

Whitney's use of the term "ghetto" is complex, in that she both argues against the stereotype that she thinks others hold about all African Americans being ghetto and also reifies that stereotype as she jokes with her sister. Though she questions its applicability to her personally, in neither instance does she seem to question the validity or use of the term.

Another distinction students drew is that between *being* black and *acting* black, with the latter defined as being ghetto. Carla first negated skin color as the definition of being black, but then highlighted that acting black is a critical component of being African American. Then she defined acting black as ghetto:

> Interviewer: What does it mean to be black?
> Carla: Dark, no not dark skin. Know a lot of light-skinned people. I don't know. I hear people say if you look dark skin, but you don't act like it, then you're not black.
> Interviewer: What does it mean to act black?
> Carla: Ghetto, like out of control, you bad. Like a lot of people do bad stuff. Usually men, ghetto, in the hood.

Similarly, Tarika highlighted the difference between being a member of the African American race (that is, having dark skin) and acting black. She also defined acting white in opposition to acting black: "Even like African American people in general consider themselves ghetto, not directly, but the race, when people [say] someone acts black, that means ghetto. Black associates itself with ghetto, ignorant. For someone to say I'm acting white they consider white people rich, you know, proper, you know. I'd rather associate myself with that rather than ghetto, acting stupid."

Given the choice between being black and ghetto and being white and "proper," Tarika would choose the latter, despite the fact that she is elsewhere quite clear about being African American. What she is noting here is likely not a real desire to be white, but rather a sense that the stereotype of what it means to be African American is less preferable than the stereotype of what it means to be white. Again, what is striking here is that Tarika does not question the validity of these narratives about race.

Other students perceived similar conflicts when it came to being viewed and viewing themselves as African Americans. Several felt that they had to choose between being an "Oreo" and being ghetto. (Being an Oreo means being black "on the outside" and white "on the inside," like an Oreo cookie.) In both instances, being an Oreo and being white required students to give up their blackness, in a sense. The definition of black as ghetto creates an identity bind for African American students such that they don't want to be ghetto, and at the same time, they don't want to disassociate with the identity of blackness, even when that identity is a stereotyped one.

Alexis and Tarika resolved this tension by taking up identities as Oreos and forgoing an identity as being authentically black:

> Alexis: 'Cause I don't fit in with people that go to Oakland schools, my parents didn't raise me to go to Catholic schools. I mean they joke around and call me an Oreo. But I just stay calm and collected. I just look at that like a compliment. I'd rather be that than be seen as rowdy and ghetto.

> Tarika: They'll be like, you're an Oreo, or I don't know. . . . I know what they mean and it doesn't really bother me. I mean, the average black person they say is ghetto and they use slang and I don't . . . and if a white person uses slang, they're trying to be black. . . . [About being called an Oreo], it doesn't bother me, it's more of a compliment. I don't want to be known as acting ghetto because it's ugly.

Alexis and Tarika hint at a purposeful crafting of identity—that they would rather be seen as an Oreo than as being ghetto—and yet they fail to fully problematize the fact that they feel compelled to make a forced choice between two negated images of black people—those of ghetto and Oreo. Students do not, for example, connect this perception of identity choices to a broader societal narrative around blackness, whiteness, and schooling. Rather, they seem to accept the forced choice as real.

Marshall tried to avoid "acting black" while still maintaining a sense of personal style and of himself as authentic; yet similar to his peers, he accepted the stereotyped definitions of blackness and "acting black":

> Interviewer: Is there something you feel that you do to act black?
>
> Marshall: I don't think there's a way you can act black. I don't know, to some people acting black means to be ghetto or to wear your clothes saggy. Me, I don't wear my clothes saggy, they be big, but they don't sag. . . . some people to act black is to wear saggy clothes and big boots and to talk like whatever, whatever. That's not me. I be me. I don't talk black or act black. I just act like me.

Marshall tries to maintain a sense of personal and racial integrity and authenticity by adhering to the style similar to other youth in his neighborhood, though he modifies the style to not be so "saggy" that he would be viewed as ghetto. Marshall is walking a fine (and somewhat slippery) identity line, as he wants to be black, but authentically so. He rejects the identity of being ghetto, and yet he accepts the way others define what ghetto is.

The History of Collective Struggle and Facing Inequality

African American students' conceptions of race were not limited to a discussion of stereotypes or being ghetto. Students also articulated the importance of past collective struggle and present-day inequalities in the experience of being African American and the magnitude of this importance for them personally. Thirty-one percent of students interviewed mentioned collective struggle and inequality as a part of the African American experience.

LaToya, Lettie, and Antonia all highlighted past or current struggles that characterize being African American in their view. LaToya argued that despite the historical wrongs committed against African Americans, it is in part her responsibility not to blame other groups for these past events:

> Africans have struggled and been through a lot; it's my job to hold up the African American name and become somebody. . . . Even though I didn't go through them [slavery], my ancestors have, and I want people to know that we're not selfish and don't hold it against people who supposedly do us wrong. So they could know that there is still somebody out there, well there are a lot of people that don't hold something against other nationalities.

LaToya makes two primary points: she references the historical struggle of African American people, and she expresses a sense of responsibility to represent African American people who don't hold grudges.

While LaToya emphasized the struggle of African Americans in the past, Lettie viewed the struggles of African Americans as being lived very much in the present:

> Interviewer: So what does being African American have to do with your experience here [at school]?
>
> Lettie: It does, it seems like a lot of the administrators . . . they'll think . . . like it seems like they be harder on you. A lot of . . . it seems like they treat you differently. Like when you bring it up you get in trouble. Like for example, they'll treat me and a Mexican like different than they treat another person, but they say like they try or they're quiet and it seems like they just want everybody to be the same, but it's like I would get in more trouble doing something than that next person doing it. . . . Say, I say a cuss word . . . and I could say it so low, right? I could be having a one-and-one conversation with somebody and they'll hear me and say "Get outside." But then they could be teaching and somebody could be like . . . they'll cuss . . . and they'll just say "Stop that" or "Don't say that word." It's like I get in more trouble when I do it, but when the next person does it, they don't get trouble, and when I bring it up they say "We're not talking about that person, we're talking about you."

Lettie focuses on her own experiences of struggle in the face of discrimination, as she explains how, in her view, school administrators are harder on African American students. She gives the example of how an African American student might be punished for a rule infraction when other students, who should have been punished, might not be.

Antonia highlighted the past struggles of African Americans but also sees those struggles as occurring in the present, both in general, in that African Americans have to struggle to get what they want, and also at school:

> Antonia: What does it mean to be black in America? It means a lot. I wouldn't say the whole racism and everything is over with, because it's not. And it's so much that we still gotta work for to get to what we want. And truthfully, I don't think that we are ever gonna reach that point. Well, not while I'm alive, and I still gotta lot more living to do, God willing, you know. But I don't think, it's sad to say, I don't think we ever gonna reach that point where we can just get somewhere in life without having to go through so many obstacles to get there, so many stereotypes, so many whatever to get there.
>
> Interviewer: Does it mean anything in particular to be black in this school?
>
> Antonia: Um . . . not really. Like, not really, I wouldn't say. I don't know. Many races are scared of black people, but I know it's like Asian people, they're like, OK, I'll do whatever you say. It's like, Why are you scared? Come on, I'm not gonna hurt you. Yeah, I'd say probably white and Asians are scared.

Antonia views being African American as having to deal with the obstacles that are mainly caused by racism, including being feared by others at school. Thus, for a third of the students interviewed in this study, being African American had much to do with managing and surviving in the face of historical and present-day racism.

Tension between Race Mattering and Not Mattering

Overall, African American students walked a potentially treacherous identity tightrope—they wanted to be black, but not too black. They were well aware of the stereotypes about them that peers and teachers carried, and they worried about being viewed as cosigners of these negative stereotypes. Moreover, they rarely questioned why stereotypes existed, and they often struggled with locating themselves within existing racial narratives. However, at the same time that students were painfully aware of the salience of race and subsequent consequences, they also minimized race in relation to their own experience, and some argued strongly that race was inconsequential to their lives at school. For instance, both Clem and Cornell said that being black didn't matter at all to their experience in school. When asked "Does it matter to be black at Washington?" Clem answered, "It don't really matter, not here it don't." In fact, 50 percent of African American students interviewed said that race did not matter in their experience in school and in society. However, of that 50 percent, almost all also reported the existence of racial stereotypes or inequities based on race.

Whitney expressed the sentiment that race doesn't matter to her experience: "Because now, I think, it's equal, everything is mixed, you see everybody's listening to everything. You can be black listening to country, you can be white listening to rap, it doesn't matter nowadays." And Malik, in answer to the question "Does it mean anything to be black at Washington?," replied: "You act just like anybody else, ain't nothing different about you. Ain't nothing different about being Mexican, black, white, black, Japanese, or whatever. People criticize and there's always gonna be racism wherever you go. But if you're gonna live in the past then do that, but in my eyes, nobody is different." These students downplay the role of race in their lives and at Washington, but they do so in contrast to other portrayals of Washington (often their own) as a place where racial stereotypes are prevalent. Malik implies that this view is not solely due to a lack of recognition of racial inequalities, but also to a perspective that argues that race *shouldn't* matter, in an ideal state of affairs.

Kathy further explained why she felt that a focus on race was inappropriate:

> A lot of black people, they feel like society owes them because of the whole slavery thing. But it's happened to everybody . . . it's happened to all races. All races have been enslaved or mistreated. Everyone has been mistreated because of the type of person or the way they are,

so I don't think that they should just, you know. I think it's serious because of what happened. But I don't think that they should still . . . you know . . . it's still . . . it's not that serious now because everybody has equal rights. Everybody gets mistreated shouldn't say 'cause because I'm black . . . you gonna treat me like whatever whatever, it's just like that for everybody. You shouldn't feel singled out. Black people shouldn't feel like they were singled out because it happened to everybody.

Kathy articulates a belief here that it is wrong for African American students to feel that society owes them something, and she sees it as important to understand that all groups have been discriminated against and have faced struggles by virtue of race. Like the racial narratives that position African Americans as potential criminals and not oriented to school, this narrative encapsulates a set of ideas about race common in our society.

Students simultaneously held perspectives about race mattering and not mattering. Furthermore, when pushed to think about the ways that racial disparities in math courses played out in their schools, African American students attributed these racial differences to individual effort or family encouragement. Consider the following:

Interviewer: Does race have anything to do with doing well in school?
Jameel: I don't think so. But it seems to be that it's true. 'Cause most of the African American kids up here, it's like they don't really—it seems to me that they don't really care about school as much as Asians or white kids who are at the school. It seems like they care less than all of them. And they not dedicated enough. Like if they hit a problem they just gonna shut down and not try to work through it. And like Asians, I have a couple Asian friends, if they get a problem, they gonna work through it until they get it right. They just—they don't stop. They dedicated.
Interviewer: Why do you think that is?
Jameel: I don't know. It probably has to do with how they raised at home or whatever. I think that's what it is. 'Cause if I get a problem I work through, so I can't say that all African Americans do that, 'cause I work through it when I get a problem.

Jameel endorses racial differences in achievement and effort but sees himself as an exception. He argues that African American students in general don't care as much about school as other groups do because they were not raised to do so. He also feels that African Americans give up too easily. This statement invokes the model-minority Asian stereotype and at the same time positions African Americans as not caring about school and unwilling to work hard to succeed.

Similarly, Shaundra attributed the low numbers of African American students in AP courses to students making choices about which courses to take:

> Interviewer: Does race have anything to do with doing well in school here?
>
> Shaundra: I think it might have a little. I just noticed like being in AP classes, it's not a lot of black kids in there. Normally it's just like me, and my twin, and like somebody else.
>
> Interviewer: What about Latino kids?
>
> Shaundra: It's not. It's mostly Asian.
>
> Interviewer: So the AP classes are mostly Asian. So why do you think that is?
>
> Shaundra: I don't know. Maybe because they [the black and Latino students] feel like they can't do good in those classes. I don't know. A lot of the people I talk to, they just don't want to take it 'cause they don't really care.
>
> Interviewer: Do you think this school gives them equal opportunities to take those classes?
>
> Shaundra: Yeah. I think it's just based on them, if they want to take them or not.

Shaundra views opportunities as being equal for African American and other students at Washington and thus sees African American students not taking AP courses as an individual choice based on how much they care about a subject rather than offerings available to them. These notions of individual effort and motivation, along with references to family support, mirror the stereotypes about African American students described in the comments from students noted above. They also take up a narrative of meritocracy—that the people who are willing to work hard get ahead—and in doing so, assume an egalitarian or color-blind school context.

OVERALL, these interviews with African American students about what it means to be African American have offered insight into the ways that some high school students think about what it means to be African American both broadly and in their school context. Students found stereotypes about being African American both salient and powerful, especially stereotypes about African Americans as being ghetto.

Students also knew that both the racial boxes and the stereotypes they encountered essentialized African Americans, but they lacked a strong sense of identity options that defined and rejected these representations. Furthermore, although students were articulate about the inequity and race-based struggle that they observed around them today and historically, they also tended to make individual attributions for these systemic issues when pressed to analyze events in their own school context. In other words, these data suggest that African American students simultaneously hold conflicting views about what it means to be African American, about whether race matters or not, about the prevalence of racial stereotypes, and about whether or not to endorse a color-blind philosophy on race. Such conflicting notions may not come as a surprise, given the conflicting views of race held in schools (Pollock, 2005) and in society more broadly (Bonilla-Silva, 2006).

Indeed, the mirroring of students' racialized narratives and the narratives that exist about race in society was striking. And yet, students were also dissatisfied with the ways they were required to take up overly constrictive or ill-fitting definitions of blackness. This came across most clearly when they described the complexity of their ethnic/racial heritage; students identified as black or African American but deemed these labels inadequate in capturing the nuance or complexity of their identities. Still, when it came to defining blackness as ghetto, students were willing to accept the essentialized racial narratives about blackness given by others, such as being willing to take up identities as Oreos to avoid being viewed as ghetto. Similarly, although African American students acknowledged racism as part of both an historical legacy and an aspect of the daily lives of African Americans, they also denied the importance of race, drawing on egalitarian and color-blind narratives to make justifications.

These data illustrate the multiple ways in which students' racialized identities were related to the racialized narratives that exist about African Americans in the broader society. In effect, these racialized and conflicting narratives became resources for the construction of identity for African American students. The data also suggest that racialized narratives are lived and enacted by multiple actors across the multiple settings of young people's lives.

Conclusion

This chapter has underscored the range of ways that the African American students featured in this study defined what it meant to be African American. Interviews with students revealed that many of them viewed being African American as involving collective struggle with both inequality and being ghetto. The interviews also showed that students were very much attuned to the negative stereotypes about African Americans that typically abound in society and in schools. Some students even felt pressure to respond to or manage these stereotypes in their lives, both in and out of school.

As Du Bois noted in 1903, and what these students have suggested remains an issue for them today, being African American in the United States means that one is constantly under threat of being framed as "a problem": the achievement problem, the neighborhood problem, and the problem with schools. This chapter has shown that African American high school students are painfully aware of this framing of members of their racial and ethnic group and that they often define themselves and their identities in the face of such strong negative stereotypes. Chapter 4 begins to explore how African American students negotiate these stereotypes and other identity options in relation to school, examining academic and racialized identity for African American high school students in an urban school and highlighting the range of ways that students interpret the relation between being a student and being African American.

Note

1. I should note that conversations about race in math classrooms were not daily occurrences, but they did happen in this classroom several times over the course of the semester. Although these incidents were not daily events, they were telling with respect to the ways students were thinking about issues of race, and I invoke this conversation here as an indication that students thought about issues of race and that stereotypes fundamentally played into their thinking.

4

On Being Black at School

coauthored by Amina Jones and Milbrey McLaughlin

THERE WERE MANY SIMILARITIES between DJ and Zeus. They were both sixteen-year-old African American males who lived in the same impoverished neighborhood and attended the same school. Both young men also struggled with school as middle school students, and both were quick-witted, with a delightful sense of humor.

But there were also profound differences between the two. DJ was on both the track and basketball teams, but Zeus didn't participate in any extracurricular activities. DJ took honors courses and planned to attend a university in the coming fall semester, but Zeus played dice in the hallway of the school during class time and questioned whether or not he would graduate from high school. DJ saw himself as a potential agent of change in a community plagued by drug sales and prostitution, but Zeus was an active participant in the street economy. DJ was able to articulate his role in and reliance on the legacy of African American scholars in the United States, but Zeus exhibited no such racial consciousness; instead, he defined his racialized identity by default on the street corner.

These two young men illustrate both the promise and the peril of life and schooling for many youth in urban schools. Like the young people in Chapter 2, DJ and Zeus engaged in multiple learning settings and communities of practice, which offered them particular kinds of resources for identity development, engagement, and learning. Like the students in Chapter 3, they worked actively to make sense of the stereotypes that other people imposed upon them in varied learning settings. In this chapter, I take a closer look at schools as complex spaces within which students both engage in the academic endeavor and construct their identities as students and as African Americans. I focus on the experiences of four students in one school, which I will call Jackson High. I use a case study approach in order to illustrate the processes of identity and engagement as they occurred in the context of the school and to highlight the nuanced and complex differences among students, across school sites, and sometimes within the same school context. I also focus on engagement in school (and to some degree achievement), rather than learning per se, though clearly learning and engagement are related. This was in part because my colleagues and I were more interested in understanding the students' connections to school in general than their learning in any particular content area.

Research on Racialized Identities and Schooling

Evidence from psychological studies shows that students' racialized identities matter for school success (Oyserman, Harrison, and Bybee, 2001; Sellers, Chavous, and Cooke, 1998). For example, Oyserman and colleagues (2001) found that when racial identity content included achievement as a part of what it meant to be black, African American students had higher levels of academic efficacy; that is, they felt that they could successfully achieve in school. Spencer and colleagues (2001) have also examined how variation in African American identities might relate to achievement. For instance, they showed that African American students who held a Eurocentric orientation had lower academic achievement and lower self-esteem than students who held a proactive Afrocentric orientation. Thus, the presence of particular racialized identity meanings seems potentially powerful for supporting academics.

Research studies in educational anthropology and sociology have also supported the notion that there are multiple ways that African American students position themselves with respect to both race and school, and that some patterns are conducive to high achievement while others are less conducive to doing well in school (Carter, 2008; Carter, 2005;

Davidson, 1996; Fordham and Ogbu, 1986; O'Connor, 1999). For example, Carter (2005), in her study of African American and Latino students, identified three categories that describe how students made sense of themselves both racially and academically: cultural mainstreamers, who assimilate to a mainstream culture; cultural straddlers, who tap into the resources of U.S. society while maintaining a strong sense of cultural identity; and noncompliant believers, who espouse an achievement ideology yet behave in resistant and oppositional ways in school. Thus, how students situate themselves racially informs how they perform in academic settings.

These studies have been critical in elucidating students' perspectives on their racialized identities and their relation to school and have pointed to interesting profiles of these beliefs and behaviors on the part of youth. However, some of this work implies that African American youth see their racialized identities, at worst, in opposition to school success, and, at best, as a cultural identity that can be straddled with an alternative identity that includes success in school. That notwithstanding, this line of research also points to the complexity and potentially local nature of the meaning that African American students ascribe to their racialized identities. For instance, some students see a lack of congruence between their racialized identities and academic achievement, and others successfully straddle a racialized identity and identity as a successful student in school.

Davidson (1996) has pointed out that racial and ethnic identities are negotiated in school and classroom contexts and that these contexts can support or fail to support the extent to which youth see school as a part of or in opposition to their racial and ethnic identities. Specifically, Davidson found that features of school contexts that contributed to manifestations of disengagement and opposition for students of color included academic tracking, negative expectations, racial discrimination, bureaucratized relationships and practices, and barriers to information. Conversely, Mehan, Hubbard, and Villanueva (1994) argue that racialized identities of marginalized students need not be defined in opposition to school success in school settings where students are expected to succeed and are given information about college and other support.

Clearly, then, one important factor in understanding racialized identities and their relation to schooling outcomes is the nature of schooling practices to which students are exposed. The idea that the school context has a significant effect on students' racialized and academic identities has been supported by theories that view the self as fluid across contexts (Markus and Kunda, 1986; Shelton and Sellers, 2000; Stryker and Serpe, 1994). Such school contexts are important in part because they provide students with different configurations of identities, through modeling, norms, and social interaction. In other words, *racial socialization* is ongoing and occurring in these school settings.

The core concern of this chapter is to highlight the diversity in the identities that African American students take up (with respect to school and race) and to examine how the academic and racialized identities that students construct are linked to their experiences and access and exposure to particular kinds of racial socialization in local school and classroom settings. I focus on two categories of students, which represent the opposite ends of a continuum: students like Zeus, who accept the narrative that being African American means being disconnected from school achievement; and students like DJ, who view their African American identity as supporting their school achievement. We call these two groups "street savvy" and "school oriented and socially conscious." These two groups of students hold quite different views of what it means to be African American and have different relationships with the stereotypes about African Americans—the street-savvy group taking up and reifying stereotypical aspects of African American identity, and the school-oriented and socially conscious group purposefully rejecting such stereotypes.

The Connected Youth Project

It is important to understand a bit about the project from which these data are drawn (see the appendix for a longer description of research methods). In 2002, my research group began a project at Jackson High School, a predominantly African American urban high school with a long history of underachievement. The focus for this research was the ways that students managed their identities as students and as African Americans; how these identity issues related to school engagement and achievement; and how the school fostered particular configurations of identity through its structure, norms, and practices.

The two-year, multimethod research project involved several layers of data collection. Because our goal was to capture student experiences and student perspectives on the role of school in their lives, we began with weekly focus groups. These groups of about ten students each met for nine weeks; during these meetings we elicited student perspectives on their school, their identities, and the role of school in their lives as well as their experiences as students in general and African American students at Jackson High in particular. Many of the focus group students were interviewed and were observed in classrooms and in other activities on the school grounds. Academic and attendance records were collected for all focus group participants. We also conducted intensive case studies with a smaller number of students (seven), who were shadowed for eight full school days. Additionally, fifteen teachers and staff members were interviewed formally, and informal conversations with teachers and staff also informed our understandings of how identities and engagement were structured and taken up at Jackson High. Finally, we surveyed 121 students to examine the relation between students' racial identities, sense of connectedness to the school, and achievement. In this chapter I draw primarily on case study, focus group, and interview data.

The School and Neighborhood Context

Jackson High School is located in East Rockland, a historic section of a large northern California city. At the time of this study, almost twenty thousand people lived in East Rockland according to the 2000 census. The population was 64 percent African American, 16 percent Latino, and 9 percent Asian and Pacific Islander. Income levels in the neighborhood were the lowest in the county. More than two-thirds of households in East Rockland earned less than $30,000 in 1999, as compared with 28 percent in the county as a whole. Half of the households in the poorest census tract earned less than $11,000 a year. Almost half (45 percent) of East Rockland residents aged twenty-five and older did not have a high school diploma, compared with 18 percent in the county as a whole.

Jackson High is one of the five traditional comprehensive high schools in the Rockland Unified School District. Though it was built in the 1930s to serve 2,400 students, Jackson was the district's smallest high school, enrolling only 670 students because of families electing to send their children to other district high schools. However, its small size permitted the school to emphasize personalization and relationships among staff and students. For the 1999–2000 school year, the pupil-to-teacher ratio was 16.2 to 1, with a reported average class size of 21.5 students. Jackson High School has struggled with chronic absenteeism as well as with difficulties in getting students to attend classes once they arrive at school. These two factors significantly affected the school climate and physical environment. Faculty and staff estimated that approximately five hundred students were present on an average school day. However, our observations left us with an even more dismal picture of attendance at Jackson: although the average class enrollment size was around twenty-five, class attendance typically averaged ten students on any given day. Students often congregated in unmonitored areas inside the stairwells, along upper floors, and outside the building.

The school had a long history of poor academic performance and struggled to improve academic achievement in the face of an alarmingly high dropout rate and test scores that were among the lowest in the state. The four-year dropout rate was 46 percent in 2000. In 2005, Jackson High graduated 33 percent of those students who matriculated as ninth graders in 2001, an increase from the previous graduating class, which represented only 15 percent of those students who matriculated as ninth graders in 2000.

Despite these challenges, a sense of "family" existed in the school, and students, staff, and faculty knew one another and greeted one another in the hallways. Additionally, at the time of our study, Jackson was in the midst of reforms to improve both its social and academic climates. Jackson High administrators created AP classes as part of their efforts to foster a more academic culture. AP classes were offered in several subjects, but because most of the students were unprepared for AP material, the courses enrolled a broad range of achievement levels and students were placed in the AP classes on the basis of their potential rather than their past achievement. Very few students (only a handful in several years) had actually passed an AP exam.

In many ways, the school constituted a unique and highly African American–centered cultural space. There was a high proportion of African

American students and faculty in the school, and the faculty often initiated conversations with students about race relations in the United States and in African American history. The school was deeply rooted in its historically African American neighborhood, such that many students came from families that had lived in East Rockland for generations and had parents and even grandparents who had attended Jackson. The main hallway was covered with a large mural that depicted African and African American historical figures, and most of the office staff were African American.

Two Configurations of Racial and Academic Identity

Our findings showed lots of variation in how students understood and expressed the nature of their African American racialized identities at Jackson, which were related to their exposure to different racial socialization practices within the school. As mentioned above, we found two versions of African American racialized identity in the study. The first consisted of a "thug" or "gangster" identity, consistent with the portrayals of black as being ghetto in Chapter 3, and included a sense of oneself as a participant in the street economy and not seeing one's African American identity as being connected to school. We called this a "street-savvy" African American identity. The other we called a "school-oriented and socially conscious" African American identity, and it involved being connected to school, community, and a cultural and historical legacy and seeing oneself as an agent for change and a positive force in the community. Though presented as distinct types for the purpose of explanation, in reality these aspects of identity might be conceptualized as particular configurations of possibilities available to students; for instance, a student might endorse some aspects of each of these, or she or he might even hold contradictory conceptions simultaneously (as illustrated in Chapter 3). In short, identity as lived is complex and fluid.

It is important to note that all the students embraced an identity as African American, though they varied with respect to the way they defined being African American. In other words, identity was racialized for all of the students; however, the nature of that racialization varied. Students also differed in their level of critical thought about their racialized identities; some students uncritically performed a racialized persona (or stereotype), while others constructed an African American identity as a product of a more thoughtful consideration of their place in the community and the world. My focus in this chapter is to illustrate variations in the African American identities that students held, to explore how this range of African American identity meanings played out in the lives of young people, and to show how these meanings were linked to the social and institutional contexts of Jackson High.

Street-Savvy African American Identity

In the street-savvy version of African American identity, being African American meant being gangster or being connected to "the street" or "the block" (the neighborhood). It also included both the speaking of AAVE and a clothing style for males that included baggy jeans, oversized T-shirts, and caps. Additionally, some students considered this street-savvy identity to be antithetical to doing well in school, but most saw it as simply being disconnected from the academic aspects of school. This way of defining African American racialized identity is most commonly represented in popular movies (for example, *ATL* and *Freedom Writers*[1]), music videos, and hip-hop and rap music (for example, 50 Cent and Too Short[2]), especially those geared toward urban African American youth (Ro, 1996). This racialized identity included viewing African Americans as drug dealers, pimps, and gangsters who are not well educated and don't care about the law, citizenship, or their futures—images consistent with students' definitions of being ghetto from Chapter 3.

Claude, a sophomore at Jackson High, typified the display of this version of African American identity. Typical of many of his classmates, he considered school to be a place for social interaction rather than for intellectual development. Claude could often be found hanging out on campus instead of going to class, sometimes shooting dice or chatting in the third-floor hallway or near the gym.

Claude was born in East Rockland and raised by his grandmother. At 5′6″ Claude was shorter than many of his peers. He hid his small frame beneath multiple layers of oversized T-shirts, jeans, and a yellow and black heavy leather coat that he wore daily and rarely removed while in the school building. He had light-brown skin, and he rarely smiled. He had a reserved nature, but his timely interjections revealed that he was a very active listener during group conversations and had a keen sense of when to speak in order to be heard. Claude came to our sessions only when his friend Zeus (a regular attendee) brought him along. While Zeus was quite talkative, Claude spoke less often. He often needed to be coaxed into staying after he finished eating the free pizza offered at the start of each focus group session. In general, he was relatively quiet as we discussed issues of teachers, school, administrators, and academics.

Claude joined the conversation only when the topic turned from school to discussions of the block, drugs, or illegal activity—he clearly identified with the "street" life. For instance, in one focus group session, researchers introduced the idea of research assistants "shadowing" the youth participating in the study. A discussion of what they do after school ensued. Claude (who had said very little the entire session) said loudly to the group that after school he goes home to call his "PO" (probation officer). Then moments later he repeated himself, "I call my PO and tell him I'm in the house." On this day and on others, Claude persisted in positioning himself as gangster and intimately connected to the block. Later in the session, the students were teasing one another, jokingly accusing each other of smoking "weed" (marijuana). There was friendly banter, with students pointing fingers, saying, "You smoke weed," "No, you smoke weed." Claude shifted the conversation from playful accusations of others to one about himself as he addressed another student, "We was smoking and drinking together, huh, Chris?" Chris replied, "Yeah." In this comment, Claude took the opportunity to again position himself as gangster and as participating in illegal activities.

The social landscape of identifying with a gangster lifestyle had an additional dimension among female students. Connie typified a female who secured her status as street savvy through her outlook and patterns of interaction, as well as through association with her boyfriend, JD, who was a well-known gangster figure and high-profile drug dealer within the community. At age sixteen, Connie was only a freshman at Jackson High. She had repeated fifth grade, and after eighth grade she had been referred to a special district program for students with significant disruptive behaviors. Faculty described this additional year of remediation classes before entering high school as a "chance to catch up for kids who act out and are not the school type." Several staff members also disclosed that they knew of Connie's long-term relationship with JD. He did not attend Jackson High, but several of his family members were students.

Connie was tall with a slender build and a rather fashionable general appearance. Like most of the other girls, she wore jeans often with color-coordinated sneakers, accessories, and tops. She did not have a large social network at Jackson, in part because she did not enter with one of the local middle school cohorts. When a guidance counselor introduced Connie to research staff, he mentioned that she was "most known to the faculty because of her discipline problems." Connie laughed in response to this statement and then dismissively said, "What do they know!" During the first five months of school Connie was suspended twice for fighting. The majority of her peers from her block knew about her relationship with JD, though she did not openly discuss it during the focus group sessions. In subsequent interviews she disclosed that both of her fights had involved female students whom she suspected of being jealous because "They always tryin' to get at me. JD's with me, but I know what they want. He ain't like these fake niggas up here [in Jackson High]." When probed further about what these girls wanted, she explained: "He gets paid and they want to roll with him like I do; for him to buy them all kinds of, well, I don't know, whatever they want." Connie did not boast about these fights but was confident that she had done what was necessary to defend her relationship and maintain her status as JD's girlfriend.

Claude, on the other hand, made sure that others knew he was knowledgeable about street activities. For instance, during one session, he looked around the room and, noting the clothing of another student, declared: "He got all that blue on, he's a Crip. He be a gang banger." This statement turned the conversation to fighting and gunplay on the street, during which Claude told the group: "I fight. I had a fight on Friday." He went on to argue that people don't often fight with their fists anymore and that guns are the preferred method of combat.

These portrayals of himself as gangster were not lost on the other students. By the end of the session, students were engaged in a heated debate about selling drugs, with Claude and Zeus arguing strongly for the merits of drug selling and corner life as a viable lifestyle, and another

student, Victor, arguing strongly against it. Claude expressed the sentiment that life was short and you never knew when you would die, so the
fact that drug dealing is a short-term career that could end in death did
not concern him. He said, "Well, I only got one life to live and I'm gonna
make it fun," and, "I don't wanna get really old." By the end of the session,
he explicitly discussed drug dealing as a potential career for himself. In a
consideration of the options available to him, Claude stated, "If I don't
go to college I ain't gonna be flippin' no burgers." Another student asked,
"So what are you going to do?" He responded, "I'm gonna be pushin' five
hundred Ki's, pushin' Ki's" (pronounced "keys," meaning kilograms of co-
caine). Victor, who argued that selling drugs is easy but managing a drug
operation is more difficult, challenged this plan. He posed mathematical
questions to Claude and Zeus about selling drugs that they couldn't answer (for example, how many grams are in a Ki?). Claude retreated and
declared: "I'm gonna be a pimp when I get older. That's quick money.
Yeah, that's easier than selling drugs." Through such statements, Claude
continually positioned himself as an insider to street life, and he seemed
to take pride in this sense of himself as cool, reckless, and tough.

In another session, students watched the movie *Paid in Full*, a story
about a young man who starts out as a good student and son and becomes
a drug dealer. The movie ends badly and is intended as a cautionary tale
about street life. Our goal in showing this film was to spark conversation
about life choices and the role of school in one's life. To our surprise,
though the film was relatively obscure, Claude and Zeus had already seen
it and told us that it was not only their favorite movie, but one they
watched at home regularly. As the movie played, they recited the characters' lines, which they had clearly memorized. Connie also embraced
the film's mixed messages about "the life." She enthusiastically engaged in
conversations about the three female characters: the girlfriend of the senior drug dealer, the mother of the main character, and his younger sister.

In a discussion following one scene in which the girlfriend of the
dealer helps him with packaging drugs, Connie was adamant that the character had made the wrong decision. She repeated several times: "I would
have said no. I would not do it." Though Connie had admitted earlier
to regularly smoking marijuana, she used this instance to make it clear
that she was not willing to participate in its distribution. She became vis-

ibly annoyed at the male students (Claude and Zeus in particular) who supported the girlfriend's decision to be part of the scene. In the session two weeks before this focus group, Connie was the first participant to justify the younger sister's decision to date a drug dealer, stating, "She want money." The other female participants were more accusatory and described the sister as lazy. Connie withdrew from the conversation as the other young women continued to criticize the sister and the mother for accepting money for groceries from the boyfriend's drug sales. Like the character in the film, Connie's mother was raising her as a single parent. An office coordinator at the school who knew Connie's mother well said that she was supportive of her daughter's relationship with JD despite the ten-year age difference and JD's criminal involvements. The coordinator believed that JD was helping to financially support Connie's family.

An important aspect of the thug or gangster identity has to do with community. Claude and Zeus saw drug dealing not just as a viable way to make money, but also as occurring within a social network with which they were familiar. They both described the personal and familial ties to the people on their blocks and described drug dealing, getting arrested, and even being shot as "putting in work" for the block and thus being accountable and giving to their community.

I should also note that Claude and Connie (and other students who subscribed to a street-savvy definition of being African American) rarely mentioned race explicitly. Might this mean that this identity for them was not racialized? Possibly. But my colleagues and I would argue that Claude's identity as a gangster and Connie's as a girlfriend of a gangster were highly racialized and reflected the versions of African American racial identity that were available to them in the local African American community (the block), in the school (through peers and in the dominant stereotypes), and in the mainstream media. It is noteworthy that this portrayal is consistent with the racialized definitions of being ghetto from Chapter 3, further supporting the notion that this version of identity was racialized. Connie and Claude and his group of friends commonly used the word "nigga" to refer to themselves and others. The common use of this word as a self-identifier also supports the notion that the gangster identity was racialized, even if the students who endorsed it did not articulate it as such. Race was also implied in Claude and Connie's identification with the block, in that in this city, neighborhoods were generally segregated by race. Claude and Connie's neighborhood was almost entirely African American. The lack of explicit discussion about race among the students may also reflect that this street-savvy identity was often less the product of thought and reflection and more a process of embracing a common narrative about African Americans.

Indeed, while students who endorsed a gangster identity rarely identified it as explicitly African American, other students openly articulated their struggles with gangster as one of multiple competing definitions of blackness in their local context. One such student was Victor (who argued with Claude about drug dealing). After attending a focus group in which we talked explicitly with students about what it meant for them to be African American, Victor pulled us aside to express the tension he felt in trying to be African American in a way that fit with his perception of what his peer group thought. Victor felt that his peers thought that being African American was about being "hard" and being "on the block" and wearing particular kinds of clothes. He said that he did not really believe that, but he found himself endorsing this characterization to fit in with this group of peers (see Chapter 5 for more about Victor's dilemma).

Connie also articulated an awareness of the variance among her definitions of being African American. In testifying to the authenticity of her boyfriend's gangster status, she often juxtaposed him with the males at her school whom she dismissively described as "stupid niggas," "fake niggas," and most frequently as "fake gangsters." Her status as "girlfriend of a gangster" depended on a perception that the intelligence and realness of her boyfriend's racialized identity involved being "on the block" and participating in the illegal dealings that had earned him his reputation and her own, by association.

Constructing Street-Savvy Identities in School   Thus far, I have focused on perceptions that Claude and Connie had of themselves in the context of community, rather than in the context of school. For Claude, the academic side of school was simply outside the scope of his definition of himself. Indeed, he rarely attended classes, never carried a pencil or backpack, and did not join any conversation in our focus groups that had to do with school or the classroom. Although Connie attended the majority of her classes—70 percent for the first semester, which was above the student average—she was noticeably disengaged on most occasions. Like several other students in her classes, she was frequently observed sitting at her desk with her head in her hands. Incidentally, both of Connie's major physical altercations with other girls had happened in the classroom.

In part, the fact that Claude and Connie took up this street-savvy identity may be related to the identities they were offered access to in their neighborhood and at school. That is, the presence of this gangster identity and the absence of a positive school identity were both supported by the school and classroom contexts in which Claude and Connie participated. One way that the gangster identity (and the lack of importance attributed to school) was made available in the school context was by a local system of tracking. At Jackson High, students experienced two very different school contexts. One offered students higher-than-average academic standards, viewed students as capable and college bound, provided information about college, and incorporated students in the leadership of the school. The other school context (the one Claude and Connie were a part of) provided students with little academic content and little information about college or even their own academic standing and requirements to graduate. These "two schools" were not different physical spaces; rather, they were two different ways that students were afforded learning opportunities and identities within the same school space. Students varied in their understanding and knowledge of these two tracks within the school, and some students moved between classes from one track and classes from the other. The AP track was relatively small, consisting of approximately 5 to 10 percent of the student population.

Claude and Connie experienced school as a place where students were largely invisible, where academic work was not demanded, and where students were allowed to fail. Moreover, students like Claude and Connie did not have access to information about graduation or college. As already noted, Claude spent most of his time during the school day wandering the hallways, in the bathroom, and socializing with friends in unmonitored areas around campus. Although Connie skipped class less frequently than Claude, her openly hostile relationship with school staff left her just as disconnected.

When they did attend class, Claude, Connie, and their peers often experienced poor or nonexistent teaching (for example, in the music class where students watched popular culture movies every day, or the Spanish class where there was a long-term substitute who rarely conducted lessons and who spoke Portuguese, but not Spanish). As noted, issues of attendance plagued this "second school," and teacher absenteeism was also quite high; students complained that teachers were not there to teach them.

The gym and the hallways were the most popular gathering spots for students who were cutting class. Physical education (PE) was scheduled as a double-period class, which made monitoring student attendance difficult and rarely attempted. Although the PE instructor typically had fifty to sixty students on the roster, there were often about thirty additional students among the group. The students not registered to attend the class would sit among the others in the bleachers and/or roam the area socializing. On one occasion, an administrator entered the gym with the intention of sending the "cutters" back to their assigned classrooms. Connie was among the students told to leave the gym, but she was actually assigned to the class for that period. She began arguing with the administrator and was sent to the principal's office. She continued using a loud tone of voice with the principal and was informed that she was being suspended. Staff who witnessed the exchange reported that Connie's aggression escalated, and as a male staff member tried to restrain her, the principal stepped in between them. During the altercation Connie hit the principal. Following a series of disciplinary-appeal hearings during which two faculty members and Connie's mother spoke in her defense, Connie was expelled from Jackson High just before the end of her freshman year.

The hallways constituted another place of constant movement and activity. In one hallway on the third floor, gambling and smoking marijuana were common during school hours. Claude was a regular participant in these activities, and his peer group consisted of others who also participated in them on the school grounds, as well as other illegal activities outside of the school. Thus, the school context supported Claude's identity as a gangster who did not participate in intellectual or academic activities. It also supported Connie's identity as a girlfriend of a gangster—perhaps in part because she too was not offered opportunities to receive high-quality instruction or to engage in a community of learners in a classroom.

In some ways, our presentation of Connie and Claude is stereo-typical and confirms much of the media's portrayals of "urban" youth. However, this consistency between their self-portrayal and the media's images of African American urban youth is an interesting point. It may be that such stereotypical portrayals do reflect the experience of some portion of the population; however, it may also be that Claude and Con-nie took up an African American racial identity that was made available to them both locally (on the block) and in the school and more broadly in society—that is, they were racially socialized in ways that conformed to a stereotypical portrayal of African Americans. I have referred to this process of students taking up the identities that they observe in the media as "identity parroting" (Nasir, 2010) to capture the ways that students can come to take up such identities uncritically.

School-Oriented and Socially Conscious African American Identity

Students who embraced the school-oriented and socially conscious African American identity were also deeply connected to their communi-ties, but their conception of what their community was and what that commitment meant was different from the conceptions of the street-savvy youth. These students held an African American identity that in-cluded a strong connection to the local, national, and historical African American community and a sense of themselves as potential agents for change in that community. This identity also included a sense of them-selves as students.

Alonzo was an eighteen-year-old senior at Jackson High, born and raised in East Rockland. He was tall and slender, with dark skin, a short haircut, and a ready smile. He carried himself with a confidence that fit his position in the school as student body president, school board student representative, salutatorian with a 3.7 grade point average, news-paper editor, and contributing member of the football and track teams. Alonzo dressed in the clothing styles typical at Jackson and in the Af-rican American community—large T-shirts and baggy jeans—and he listened to popular hip-hop and rhythm and blues music. On several occasions, he wore oversized T-shirts or sweatshirts bearing the logos of local universities. When talking to friends (and sometimes in class), he often used AAVE.

For Alonzo, his community included his family, the East Rockland community, and the African American community, locally, nationally, and historically. This sense of community was reflected in the way he framed his family's connection to Jackson High: "There's a rich family history here [at Jackson]. My grandmother went here and my grandfather, my aunties and uncles." His senior project (a research paper mandatory for graduation) documented the history of African Americans in the city of Rockland. On one of our first encounters with him, Alonzo gave our research staff a guided tour of his evolving portfolio, pointing out pictures of Jackie Robinson and other historical African American figures with a sense of expertise and pride. In an interview he told us that he aspired to be the mayor of Rockland after completing his undergraduate and graduate education.

Similarly, Adrienne, who ranked in the top five of her class, had taken seven AP classes by her senior year. Her mature demeanor, combined with her tall height and heavy-set frame, made her appear older than she was, though her candor, high energy, and curiosity were quite fitting for her seventeen years. She often wore jeans and T-shirts bearing African-centered or college words or logos.

Like Alonzo, Adrienne took initiative regarding her learning. In class she was the first to raise her hand, and she asked questions when she didn't understand something. Her English teacher described her as "the type of person who is willing to push herself to academic success." She aspired to be a child psychologist—an interest that was sparked by her experience in a peer educator program. She also planned to write inspirational books for youth to encourage them. "Just being in the East Rockland community . . . life is hard," she said. "It's hard at home and it's hard at school. I just want to speak to people and help young people understand that I know it's hard but you have to have a positive outlook." Thus Adrienne, like Alonzo, aspired to be a positive agent for change in East Rockland and saw herself as a part of this community.

While Adrienne said that she had always been self-motivated,

Alonzo noted that he had not always held such lofty goals. He said that in ninth and tenth grades he wanted to play basketball:

> I thought all I wanted to do was play basketball. Yet my mind sort of shifted because I [*pause*] I used to want to go to the NBA and stuff, and I had my other dreams I wanted that were like in-the-closet dreams, though. I knew what I wanted to do. I knew I wanted to write. I knew I liked politics. I knew . . . I knew that I wanted to do those things, but I was kind of . . . I kind of got stuck in a dream of being an NBA player. Because you know, its hard, society pushes black kids . . . that's all you can do. That's all you can do.

In this reflection, Alonzo articulates both a change for him over time in his goals, and the way that society "pushes" African American youth into particular pathways, such as sports, perhaps referring to prevalent stereotypes about African American students. Alonzo decided instead to pursue writing and politics through his involvement in school organizations such as student government and the school newspaper.

Observations on multiple occasions indicated the congruence of Alonzo's racialized and academic selves. For instance, one morning he attended an English class where the teacher was not present. He explained to researchers that the teacher was proctoring the AP English exam and that students were to work on their senior projects unsupervised. Twelve students came to class and sat down to work independently, playing a hip-hop CD and talking to one another while they worked. The conversation took place almost entirely in AAVE, and occasionally a student danced a little to the music. Alonzo and two friends (all African American males) sat at a table together. One of the students said, "I can't concentrate with it that loud" and turned down the music a bit.

At one point their conversation turned to the topic of filling out scholarship applications, and they discussed how they considered filling out such applications as a good use of time. They even updated each other on the scholarships they were currently working on. One student said, "If you'll give me $2,000 to write an essay, I'll have it to you the next day." A joke sprouted up when Alonzo accused another student of "side dealin'"—a term that Alonzo invented meaning applying for a scholarship but not bringing it to the attention of one's friends. This would theoretically increase one's individual chances of receiving the money without competition, but he viewed this practice as having a negative effect on the overall welfare of the group. They also used "side dealin'" to refer to a teacher who gave scholarship opportunities only to some students at the expense of others. This term illustrates the incorporation of Alonzo's racialized identity and his academic identity in that he coined a slang term to talk about an academic subject like applying for scholarships. Interestingly, the term sounds like the term "drug dealin'," which is used to describe street activity.

Alonzo's focus on academic activity was evidence of his view of himself as a part of the historical legacy of his family and the African American community and his desire to make his community a more positive place (this is what motivated his aspirations toward becoming mayor). He knew that drug dealing existed as an option in his community, but he saw those who chose that path as "followers." In an interview, he said: "I consider people who sell drugs to be followers. A lot of people who sell drugs just doing it because they come from East Rockland, they may have seen their brother or uncle or dad doing it, so then they want to do it." Adrienne expressed similar views about the effect of drugs in her community. In response to viewing the same movie during which Zeus and Claude celebrated the drug-dealing activities of the central characters, Adrienne was quite critical. She and Alonzo challenged the drug dealers' motives in "frontin' money" to family members and neighbors. Adrienne suggested: "But if you think about it he's not really even giving back to the community because his profit is coming from him making the community go down. Selling all them drugs to all those people." She expressed a similar disdain when commenting on other students who were not making the most of the educational opportunities at Jackson High. In a session where Adrienne identified the positive and negative aspects of the school, she highlighted students in the hallway during class and linked the school's attendance problems to reductions in funding for various advanced and elective classes.

Hence, Adrienne and Alonzo embraced a definition of what it meant to be African American that incorporated both a commitment to community embedded within a rich cultural history and a commitment to their own education. This congruence was more than just a fluid moving back and forth between conflicting identities, or seeing two identities as compatible; it was a bending of identities, such that one implied the other. Because they viewed being African American as being committed to the positive development of family and community, a strong academic identity became a part of their racialized identities.

The academic success that Alonzo and his friends and Adrienne found at Jackson did not come at the expense of being "cool" or belonging. Indeed, Alonzo was very much at the social center of the school community and had a wide range of friends and associates. Similarly, when Adrienne walked down the hall, the walk was peppered with hugs and hellos from friends as well as teachers and administrators. Other students in this school-oriented and socially conscious group also played sports or were cheerleaders or were otherwise active on the campus social scene. As we noted, both Alonzo and Adrienne spoke AAVE and wore the typical popular styles of clothing, though sometimes with African-centered slogans or college logos on the T-shirts. These styles and interactional forms were common for students who fit this identity type. While Alonzo and Adrienne were central to the Jackson High social scene, their friendship groups differed from Connie and Claude's group. Given that, although they were not considered "nerds" or Oreos, they may not have been considered "cool" by Claude and Connie's social group because of a different set of norms and expectations for behavior. Late in the spring of his senior year, for instance, Alonzo was accepted to a prestigious university in the area for the following fall. The administration and the school community celebrated his accomplishment. Adrienne and two of her classmates were admitted to the same university the following year.

The schooling and classroom environments in which Alonzo and Adrienne participated supported their identities as both racially conscious and strong students. They were a part of the AP track at Jackson, which created a very different set of experiences and opportunities for identity construction than the track that Claude was a part of. Alonzo was identified early in his high school career as a student who had "potential" and was placed in the AP track. Adrienne was also placed in the AP track by her ninth-grade counselor. While she acknowledged that AP classes were open to a range of students, she clearly considered herself a strong student. She said: "This year, they put a lot more people in AP that weren't ready for it. I think they just did it because Jackson was getting so much bad publicity. They were saying stuff about how we don't have a lot of AP classes and that students weren't really succeeding."

As a junior and again as a senior, both Alonzo and Adrienne had access (and a key) to the "college room" as well as information about college and scholarships. Students in the AP track had close relationships with teachers that centered on academic mentoring, and faculty purposely created such relationships (in the form of an informal mentoring program) to support students' academic achievement. In the spring of Adrienne's junior year, a teacher who also volunteered as the school's scholarship liaison approached Adrienne and later arranged for her to meet with the admissions outreach representative from the local university. The guidance office did not distribute this information, nor did it offer coaching to the general student population on how to prepare applications. Adrienne and a small group of her peers at the top of their class met regularly with this teacher to draft their college essays and share information about local scholarship opportunities. Those who formed these close relationships with staff early in their academic careers, most often through the summer program or through developing personal connections with staff, were placed in upper-level courses. As one student reflected:

> The AP classes here are different from any other school in the sense that a lot of African American students don't have the chance to say "I want to be in AP classes" . . . to just say "I want to be in there so I'm going to be in there." In a lot of other places students have to go through a lot of tests and everything just to get into an AP class. Whereas [at Jackson] if he wanted to be in AP English they would have been able to get in. So I told my friends about it.

Thus, the AP track served as a way for students to create experiences that supported both academic development and their identities as students. For those on the AP leadership track, the school was a place where they could feel good about being students.

The teachers who taught AP courses were largely African American, and the content of the AP history class often touched on issues of African

American history. In this way, students were encouraged through these practices of racial socialization to tie their developing academic knowledge to a cultural history of African Americans. Thus, for Alonzo and Adrienne, resources in the school context were available to support a racialized identity linked to history and school success.

Conclusion

The presence of these two identity types—street-savvy and school-oriented and socially conscious—brings to the fore several important issues. First, our data highlight that similar to other recent studies of urban, African American students (Carter, 2005; Oyserman, Harrison, and Bybee, 2001), Alonzo and Adrienne did not have to "act white" or be Oreos to succeed academically. Rather, they were able to maintain a strong sense of themselves as part of an historical legacy of African Americans, and they drew on that to support their academic achievement. Furthermore, they did not have to give up being "cool" to succeed academically. In fact, Alonzo and his small circle of high-achieving friends as well as Adrienne were highly involved in the local school community and participated in student government, the school newspaper, sports, and peer tutoring. Adrienne and Alonzo were friendly with other high-achieving students, as well as with low-achieving students, and they saw themselves as people who were "cool with" everyone at the school. They had wide friendship networks and were well liked across achievement levels. These data also suggest that not only were Alonzo and Adrienne able to blend both strong school identities and strong racial identities, but their identification with school became a part of their definition of what it means to be African American.

Second, findings show that African American speech and clothing styles were not related to orientations toward school. All of the students consistently used AAVE; listened to rap, rhythm and blues, and hip-hop music; and wore the latest urban clothing styles. However, school-oriented and socially conscious students often wore T-shirts with slogans or logos that expressed an Afrocentric perspective or were linked to colleges.

Third, it is important to remember that the identities that all of the students expressed were supported and made available to them through the local community and school contexts, which served important racial socialization functions. In part, Alonzo and Adrienne were able to maintain a definition of being African American that included high achievement and racial consciousness because they were in a local school context where the majority of the student body was African American and where they were not required to choose between being African American and being high achieving. At Jackson, students did not need to "straddle" two cultures because, similar to the out-of-school practices explored in Chapter 2, it was an inherently African American institution. Related to this is the fact that Alonzo was part of a small group of peers who supported one another in their definition of African American racial identity, as well as in the practical aspects of school, such as scholarship and college applications.

Fourth, the findings that street-savvy youth were less aware of themselves racially and what that means in social, political, and historical contexts further underscore the contentious relation between racialized and academic selves. While Alonzo and Adrienne were aware of local and national African American history and saw themselves as potential positive agents for change in their community, Claude and Connie did not display an interest in or knowledge of African American history. This may confirm findings in the literature which show that Afrocentric identities are protective and supportive of school success (Spencer et al., 2001).

Findings also illustrate that all students were connected to their communities, yet they defined those communities quite differently. Alonzo's and Adrienne's communities included their families, school community, and the local and national African American community. Claude's and Connie's communities were defined by their block, or neighborhood, which coincided with a particular drug turf. Within each of these communities, young people were racially socialized in different ways. And although all of these students were committed to their communities, that commitment meant something different, too. For Alonzo and Adrienne it meant finding ways to improve the quality of living for all in the community; and for Claude and Connie, it meant "putting in work" and putting oneself at risk for the profit of others on the block, and being loyal to others on the block.

These divergent identities were not constructed in a vacuum; rather, they reflected the types of learning experiences and racial socialization practices that students had access to and the opportunities they were afforded. Thus, these identity choices on the part of youth were grounded in their experiences in school environments. Alonzo and Adrienne were offered a school context that affirmed the importance of the cultural history of African Americans and gave them multiple messages about the possibility of academic success and college attendance. Claude and Connie, on the other hand, were not offered such opportunities to develop a sense of academic possibilities and did not experience high-quality teaching or high expectations. Such findings confirm the already strong literature on the negative effects of tracking (Gamoran, 1987; Oakes, 2004). Of course, the school was not the only source of influence on these students; their neighborhoods and families also greatly mattered in the ways the students came to see themselves and the opportunities they saw as possibilities for their futures.

Students at Jackson High could both embrace a strong African American identity and be successful academically. Furthermore, findings illustrate that academic achievement was a part of the very definition of being African American for some students. This finding adds a level of nuance to our understanding of racialized identities. Simply knowing the strength of one's sense of being African American does not determine the content or meaning of that identity, though it may be that the racial identity meanings that students held were more likely to exert an effect on achievement if the students also identified strongly with being African American. This indicates the need to consider both the strength of one's identity, the local identity meanings, and the access to racial socialization practices that students are constructing together and managing.

In Chapter 1, I noted that the research findings were mixed on the question of whether strong African American identities support or hinder achievement and academic outcomes. The data presented in this chapter suggest that certain types of African American identities may support academic achievement in school while other types may not. They also suggest that it is important to attend to the ways that our society conveys identity meanings, in the form of stereotypes, to African American students.

In this chapter, I highlighted two categories of African American identity at each end of the spectrum with respect to students' racialized and academic identities. In Chapter 5, I problematize these categories and consider youth who don't fit neatly into either type. In doing so, I engage a discussion of the specific kinds of resources for identity that learning settings in school can offer.

Notes

Portions of this chapter are adapted from N. Nasir, A. Jones, and M. McLaughlin, "What does it mean to be African American? Constructions of racial/ethnic identity and school performance in an urban public high school," *American Educational Research Journal*, 46:1 (2009): 73–114, used with permission of Sage/Society.

1. These two popular movies depict African Americans primarily as thugs and gangsters.

2. These two rap artists (both ex–drug dealers) embody stereotypes of African Americans, both in their music and in their self-presentation.

5

Caught between Worlds

IN CHAPTER 4, I identified two distinct patterns of African American identity and the ways each was supported in the local school context. Now I turn attention to the complexity of how these categories were lived and enacted in the lives of students. Specifically, I explore the identities and engagement of students who take up multiple and sometimes conflicting identities. I am mainly concerned with understanding the nature of students' identities as students, learners, and African Americans and how learning settings make identities available to them.

This chapter focuses more closely on the experiences of three students in particular, two of whom are cases drawn from the same study as that described in Chapter 4. The third student is a male track athlete drawn from the study on track briefly described in Chapter 2. I have deliberately included data on students who have conflicting identities in school as well as a student who has conflicting identities in an out-of-school learning setting; the contrast is intended to support an understanding of the complexity of these learning and identity processes in multiple kinds of settings and to avoid oversimplified comparisons of the nature of learning and identity in school versus the nature of learning and identity in practices outside of school.

The first case presented is that of Victor, who was briefly introduced in Chapter 1 and also appeared in Chapter 4. He was torn between an identity as the "hard" African American male that he felt others expected him to be and an identity as a college-bound student. The second student is Jasmine, who straddled both a "street" world and a school world; she saw herself at times as belonging in both and at other times as belonging in neither. The third case describes the experiences of Gozi, who had conflicting identities as a track athlete and as a basketball player. As I present these cases, I attend to the role of context in the identity choices that Victor, Jasmine, and Gozi perceived to be available to them. This chapter presents detailed case data on each of these students, with the purpose of elaborating how learning settings offer certain kinds of *identity resources*. In other words, I underline particular ways that aspects of the learning settings make some identities available to students, while constraining other identities.

I stress three kinds of resources: material resources, relational resources, and ideational resources. By *material resources*, I mean the ways that the physical environment, its organization, and the artifacts in it support one's sense of connection to a practice. *Relational resources* refer to the way in which positive relationships with others in the context can increase one's connection to a practice. *Ideational resources* refer to the ideas about oneself and one's relationship to and place in a practice and the world, as well as ideas about what is valued and what is good. For the students I describe in this chapter, individual choice and agency interact with the offering of these resources in complex ways.

Victor and Jasmine managed conflicting identities in school, and Gozi managed conflicting identities as he participated in track and field. These students were all struggling to define themselves in relation to a learning setting, and in doing so they straddled two potentially conflicting or incongruent identities. As I describe each of these youths, I draw attention to how the practices in which they were engaged made certain identity resources more or less available to them.

Conflicting Identities in School: Victor and Jasmine
Victor: Searching for Authenticity, Struggling with Achievement

Victor, introduced in Chapter 1, enjoyed conversation and ideas and had a ready smile. He was quick to share an interesting theory about why many students at Jackson High weren't doing well or about why black people needed to be more connected to their history. He related well to his peers across many social groups and achievement levels.

Victor had a long history of participation in community-based programs (as a sophomore he was chosen as the school's representative in a national leadership conference) and often expressed strong socially conscious opinions. One example of this, presented in Chapter 4, was his disagreement with Claude when Victor challenged the idea that illegal activity was an acceptable lifestyle and argued that drug dealing was detrimental to the African American community. In discussions, Victor often criticized both schools and societal structures. He also regularly challenged teachers in class and was highly critical of what he felt was substandard teaching. "Instead of trying to make sure you're on your task," he said of some teachers, "they'll kind of give up on you. They'll base you on a stereotype, already thinking like 'you're gonna fail so get out of my class' type of thing." He credited his critiques of the social context and of the school to conversations with his father.

Victor talked explicitly about feeling pressured by his social context to embrace a street-savvy identity, which he found to be incompatible with his social consciousness, in part because he viewed being African American (like Alonzo and Adrienne) as involving pride in one's history and a commitment to one's community. He saw his race as affirming and positive, and yet he was concerned about his odds for success and survival as an African American man in the United States. Thus, Victor clearly saw being African American in conflicting ways. In observations and interviews, he expressed both views. In one interaction during class, Victor was talking to a girl whose family emigrated from Ethiopia. After revealing that she was from Africa, she quickly (and defensively) asked him not to make fun of her because she was African. Victor responded, "I'm black! Why would I make fun of Africa?!" In this exchange, he signals his connection to a history rooted in Africa; however, he also acknowledged that being African American can involve struggle, when he said: "Coming to Jackson, I'm well aware of where I stand as a black man. I'm well aware of the chances that I've been given and what I'm deprived from, who I have to compete against. I haven't had the best of academics."

Victor sees that structural inequalities may be barriers to his future success and that he faces these barriers in part because he is African American. At the same time, he also criticizes some of his fellow

African American students who he feels have accepted a subjugated position in society and have agreed to a "thug" identity uncritically. We asked Victor about the series of focus groups he had attended over the course of the previous year of our project. He said he was frustrated with the groups because the other students made it difficult for him to express his views: "Their mentality was like, once you're in the hood, you're stuck there. Because I was talking about things that didn't match with their mentality, they said I wasn't from the hood. I had a lot to say about that, my themes and stuff. But they didn't want to hear it."

Here, Victor points out that his affiliation with the "hood" is challenged when he expresses views that are different from the "hood mentality" that the other students have. Victor's views on what it means to be black are very much aligned with the school-oriented and socially conscious students described in Chapter 4, except that he is concerned about being too different from his more street-savvy peer group and feels a pull toward adopting the street-savvy identity that he thinks others expect of him. Thus, Victor feels caught between an African American identity that is imposed on him by the popular media and his peers and a more socially conscious African American identity that does not conform to these stereotypes.

Academically, Victor had some access to identity resources that would support a school-oriented identity. Early in his high school career, he described himself as academically strong. He was placed in many AP and other high-level classes, including AP English, chemistry, and advanced algebra/trigonometry. This course placement might constitute a kind of ideational resource—that is, support for thinking about himself as a student—as well as a material resource. Victor's peer group was wide-ranging, but he saw himself as part of the more academically successful group of students. So, he also seemed to have more relational resources for a school-oriented identity; and the other students in his social network shared strong identities as students. His grade point averages in the ninth and tenth grades were 2.8 and 2.9, respectively. In our initial interactions with him, when he was an eleventh grader, he identified himself as different from the lower-achieving students in his focus group, though one or two of them were his friends. The following excerpt from field notes taken early in the first year of the project, as we were recruiting students for a focus group of "disconnected" students, shows that the school counselor saw Victor as a high-achieving student:

> Andre (a student) approached me with his friend (Victor) who said he was interested in joining the project and participating in focus groups. I gave Victor a permission form and invited him to attend the Monday meeting. I stopped in to see [the school counselor] and told him about Victor joining the group, and [the counselor] said he "is not the type of student you are targeting." He explained that Victor is probably in the top 30 of his junior class and that he should add a mix to the group.

Since the counselor assumed we were targeting low-achieving students, he defined Victor as "not the type" of student we were looking for, which indicated to us that Victor was not seen as a part of this group.

In another early set of field notes of "emerging profiles" of students in the focus groups, Victor was again positioned as a high achiever: "Victor is in the top 30 of his class and participates in several after school activities (photography, youth sounds) and community groups. He is very articulate about his decisions to do well in school and the people who have supported him in his success (i.e. his family)." Victor's class attendance, while not impeccable, was very good by Jackson standards (he attended classes 75 percent of the time during a random week we sampled). His goal was to attend a local university and major in architecture, and he maintained strong ties with an academically oriented social network. Taken together, these goals evidence the relational (membership in the academically oriented peer group), ideational (where he and others thought about him as a strong student), and material (enrollment in college preparatory classes) resources for a school-oriented identity that still seemed in place for Victor.

As a senior, Victor maintained higher-than-average attendance, though he missed an average of twenty class sessions from each of his classes over the course of the year. However, his participation (both in school activities and in the classroom) became more marginal. For instance, in one observation, he went to all of his classes but sat at a table away from his peers and either put his head down on the table or made conversation with the researcher (asking her to teach him vocabulary words). This might suggest that he still had access to the material and ideational resources of himself as a student but that he chose not to take up these identity resources. The picture proved to be a bit more complex.

Several weeks into the fall semester of his senior year, Victor was transferred from regular history to AP history. He did not do well in the course. By November, he was critical of the institution for transferring him into an AP class without the support he felt he needed to be successful, and he became discouraged academically.

> Victor: The reason why I'm slacking off now is because I don't get it. It's like, I can't read a book from the middle. Like with my AP government class, I got there late so I'm already behind. It's hard to do harder stuff to catch up. . . . I don't understand though, I should be able to catch up but I don't. . . . I gave up, but I don't want to fail so I just float by. . . . At the end of the day, I felt like I was still stupid. So, why feel stupid when you can be stupid? So that's what I'm doing.

His grade point average dropped to 1.8, his critiques of the structural inefficiencies of the school intensified, and he began to express disenchantment with school as a means to a brighter future. He talked about high school as not being relevant to his career interests in film. It seems that although Victor had access to material resources to support a school-oriented identity, he was unable to fully engage these resources because he was not academically prepared to do so. Thus, Victor experienced placement in the AP course not as a resource, but rather as an ideational liability because of the series of events that ensued. Furthermore, perhaps partly because he was not successful in AP history, Victor no longer felt that he belonged in the social network of students who were academically successful—his inability to take up the material resource of placement in the AP track had implications for the relational resources of the academically oriented friendship group. His experience in AP history also had lasting effects on his academic progress. After failing the class his first semester, Victor asked to be transferred out of the class to avoid failing it again, but the school resisted. He was finally able to transfer out of AP after having his mother write a letter making the request. By then, however, the F grade on Victor's transcript meant that he was just shy of the number of units that he needed to graduate. This F constituted both an ideational and material limitation for Victor, as it limited his future academic opportunities and caused him to doubt himself as a student. He said: "I heard last year, seniors didn't get to walk the stage because of one class. Now I see what they are talking about."

When asked about what was happening with Victor, the guidance counselor attributed his failure to a lack of motivation. She said: "He didn't pass the AP class because he didn't put in the work. If he would have done the work, he probably would have passed the class." She interpreted this as evidence of Victor not taking full advantage of the material resource of the AP class. When Victor was asked why he did not drop the class sooner, he explained that he thought staying in would help him get into college (even if the grade resulted in an F, it was still AP).

By the spring of his senior year, Victor's critiques of both the academic guidance he was receiving and the quality of instruction at the school intensified significantly. His participation in class vacillated between being engaged and involved and being completely disconnected. Consider the following excerpt from a classroom observation of Victor:

> I was escorted to Victor's second block class, Spanish III and found him watching a movie. The few students that were in class were watching a Denzel Washington movie with Spanish subtitles. A few of the girls flipped through a fashion magazine looking for the perfect hairstyle. The teacher walked in and out of the room filling his water bottle. . . . Occasionally the teacher would ask a question as to what was occurring in the movie. Victor was quick to guess the next sequence of events and figure out the plot of the movie.

Very little instruction seemed to be occurring in this class. This lack of instruction was exacerbated by the fact that this was the Spanish III course taught by a long-term substitute who did not know Spanish, as described in Chapter 4. These classroom spaces were limited with respect to material resources for *learning*, and thus for identity as a student as well. In Victor's chemistry class on the same day, only four or five students were present when the bell rang, and seven others entered after the second bell. Victor stated (to the room of students in general): "I'm taking notes this time! I'm not going to be a butthead today." He took out a pencil and notebook and began to copy down the chemistry problems that the teacher was working through on the overhead. With this declaration and subsequent display, Victor drew on a purposefully crafted ideational resource—the image of himself as not being a "butt-head." Within ten minutes, however, Victor announced that he didn't understand anything the teacher was doing and said, "I don't know what I'm writing down!" He then gave up and proceeded to chat with those around him for the remainder of the class period. On another day in that same chemistry class, students did not seem to notice when the teacher began the lesson; accordingly, student chatter continued throughout the class period. One researcher noticed that Victor looked sleepy and asked him whether he was tired. Victor responded, "Yeah, tired of this school." While Victor attempted to invoke an ideational resource to support a student identity, the lack of material resources to support that identity was too strong. So he ultimately disengaged.

Victor's spotty participation and elements of the schooling environment to which he was responding were also evident in his intermediate algebra class. Like the Spanish class, the math class was being taught by a substitute teacher (the lack of a permanent and qualified teacher could be thought of as the absence of a material resource). Victor said that the class was disorganized and that everyone got incompletes for the last marking period because they didn't have a consistent teacher. The school had gone through five different substitutes since the beginning of the school year. According to Victor, students didn't do their work in the class because they knew they were going to get incompletes.

In this class, Victor moved in and out of active participation, solving problems one minute and chatting the next. When asked whether he liked math, Victor said: "I like math, but I don't like the way it's being served. I find it unattractive." He felt that both school and math were "irrelevant" for what he wanted to do in the future. The nature of instruction in Victor's classes at Jackson did not offer much in the way of material resources that would support learning. He felt that he was a good student by the school's standards; however, eventually Victor had little confidence in his ability to graduate and attend college. The following is from a field note in early December of his senior year:

> Today Victor sounded like he had given up on his future. He said he feels like he has no options for going to college. He told me that

he scored low on the ACT [college entrance exam]. He has a 2.3 GPA. Then he missed the deadline for applying to UC schools so all he can do now is go to a junior college. I told him that he should look into schools outside of California. But he doesn't want to go out-of-state because he doesn't want to be "broke" so far from home.

At the same time, Victor also felt that he had a responsibility to be successful in order to be a positive role model for his younger brothers and sisters, saying, "I'm the one showing them that they can be successful through school and be what they want to be. So, I have to be a positive role model. I have to make it and tell them that school is good. I have no guidance, and yet I have so much responsibility. I haven't seen anyone doing what I want to do before."

By the spring, Victor was clear that he did not feel he had been adequately prepared for college and he was worried that he could not compete with students from other schools and communities for college admission. He said outright, "I don't think I'd last long or do good enough for a four-year college." Moreover, it was unclear whether he would graduate in June.

While on one hand, Victor had access to material, ideational, and relational resources to support a school-oriented identity, there were also significant barriers to these identity resources, especially the AP history course fiasco and its pivotal role in redefining Victor's academic trajectory and sense of himself as a student. Victor was also conflicted about taking up the identity that he felt was widely available both in broader society and in his peer group—that of a street-oriented, "hard" African American thug. The ideas and expectations with respect to this hard identity constituted an ideational resource. And finally, it is noteworthy that Victor had limited access to material learning resources, which also affected his sense of identity as a student and his judgments about his academic future.

Jasmine: Street Smart and Princeton Bound

While Victor was caught between his past performance as a strong student and a future he was unsure about, Jasmine was caught between a student identity and a street-savvy identity. A fair-skinned African American girl with a clear, strong voice, Jasmine often wore a terry cloth sweatsuit with her straight hair pulled back into a ponytail or bun and the latest trend in glasses. She was also a member of the track team and competed in long-distance events. One of her teachers described her as possessing a maturity beyond her age, which may have stemmed from her troubled childhood. Both of her parents were drug addicts, and she herself used drugs heavily in ninth and tenth grades. Perhaps a school administrator summed up Jasmine's situation best: "Any bad thing you can think of that can happen to a female teenager in the inner-city, it has happened to Jasmine. She dabbled in prostitution. She's been raped." Because of her parents' drug addiction, Jasmine lived with her grandmother. She said, "I'm my own parent!" Her English teacher noted her high level of responsibility and inner drive when he said: "The thing about Jasmine is that this sister keeps her head up so high. All she talks about is furthering her education despite everything she's been through."

When asked, in her junior year, what her teachers would say about her academic performance, Jasmine stated that they would say she had "improved." She reported having difficult freshman and sophomore years but was adamant about being a successful student as a junior and senior. As a senior she said: "I'm on the honor roll for the second marking period. I'm in my second year of foreign language. I'm in American government and econ, math and English 4. I'm focused on keeping my grades up and don't fall behind, which I have. I'm not worried about it, but you never know. Something could always go wrong." This sense of herself as a strong student with good grades constituted an ideational resource. Yet her recognition that "something could always go wrong" may be an indication of a conflicting ideational resource—a potential fear of falling into old patterns.

Though she didn't see herself as having strong connections with teachers at Jackson High in general, Jasmine was savvy about building good relationships with her teachers. She said that teachers were "like your second parent . . . if you can't talk to your parents, I'm pretty sure it's a teacher here you feel comfortable talking to." She felt close to two adults at Jackson: Gray, the attendance clerk and general support person, and Dr. Davis, the study skills teacher. Both of these adults supported Jasmine personally and academically, and their presence in her school life was a relational resource for a school-oriented identity. When Jasmine became pregnant in the twelfth grade, Dr. Davis offered to take her into her home and pay for her to go to college; Jasmine declined the offer in order to remain independent. She said: "Nobody never gave me nothing so I want to work for everything I get. I don't want to live with nobody. I want my own house, my own car, my own degrees, my own job, so I can say I did that." This might be conceptualized as a potential material resource—one that Jasmine elects not to take up. Gray's office was a regular hangout for Jasmine, and during her pregnancy, Gray brought her something to eat every morning, usually fruit, because he was concerned about the baby's nutrition. Other teachers were also supportive. For instance, one teacher helped Jasmine develop an individual work schedule so she would not fall behind in classes. These are both examples of material and relational resources.

Support from teachers and staff for Jasmine ranged from academic support to personal support. In one instance of both academic and personal support, Jasmine was a part of an impromptu advice session for several young women that was facilitated by a student from a local university and arranged by Ms. Shelton, the history teacher. The high school students were asking the college students questions such as, What is your university like? What is your major? Do you like the Bay Area? Then Ms. Shelton asked, "Do you have a boyfriend?" The girls all laughed at the question, and Jasmine responded, "Dang, Ms. Shelton, that's your favorite question!" Another student asserted, "What does it matter if you don't let your relationship take over your life?" Ms. Shelton responded, "It's not the fact of having a boyfriend, it's the no-good ones that I'm concerned about." Jasmine sighed, "Here we go . . ." It may be that Jasmine felt this comment to be directed toward her, given that Ms. Shelton viewed her boyfriend as "no good." This comment and the general point that the girls should choose partners who do not stand in the way of their academic trajectory can be seen as an ideational resource in support of a school-oriented identity. Thus, Jasmine garners quite a bit of support from teachers and staff—ranging from personal support that stemmed from the "familylike" atmosphere at Jackson, and academic support that was an indication of Jasmine's partial membership in the college-bound track.

Later in the same conversation, the group talked about the bad food available at Jackson and in the surrounding neighborhood. The university student said that the food at her university was very good, and she told the girls about the many food options available there. Jasmine replied, "It could never be like that here; I can't wait to get to Princeton." In this comment, Jasmine signals an ideational resource, not only a desire for the "higher end" of things in general, but also a conception of herself as a future Princeton student.

As already noted, Jasmine had a strong commitment to academics and a strong sense of herself as a student. This identity was evident in observations of her in class, both before and during her pregnancy. Jasmine repeatedly demonstrated her commitment to her schoolwork, working on problem sets or Spanish translations even when other students were not paying attention, and demanding help from teachers whenever she didn't understand something. In one observation, during an intermediate algebra class, the teacher stopped the lesson to walk over to help an individual student at her desk. Jasmine yelled out, "Keep teaching us!" When other students were late to class or were disruptive, Jasmine scolded them (often asking, "Why were you late?") and reminded them of her desire to learn. She prided herself on the way that she took initiative over her own learning and reported that she not only kept up with her schoolwork, but she also knew how many units she had completed and what classes she needed to graduate. At times, she left classes that she viewed as being unproductive to complete work for other classes. In these instances, Jasmine acted with agency to maximize her learning, even given the sometimes meager resources for learning that were available to her.

Jasmine felt confident that her pregnancy would not interfere with her academic plans. Most of her pregnant friends had dropped out of school before they had their babies, but she planned to have her baby during the winter break (the baby was due January 23) and return to school afterwards. The guidance counselor suggested that she go to a facility for pregnant teens called Bay Area Prenatal School, but she wanted her diploma to be from Jackson High. Here, Jasmine overrode what could have been a relational resource *not* in support of her school identity. She arranged for her aunt to take care of the baby during the day while she was in school, and explained her plans to continue school:

> I'm like, OK, if I'm doing good, I'm pregnant, I have all my credits, what does that tell you? I'm gonna keep going. I got all my motivation.

I got everything I need to know. I got my requirements. So what does that tell you? I'm not gonna let everything I worked hard at for four years go to waste! I'm gonna put it to use! I'm not gonna just let it sit on the shelf!

Like Connie's boyfriend from Chapter 4, the baby's father was a local drug dealer and gangster who was also seventeen years old. In the fall of Jasmine's senior year, he had just been released from a brief stint in the local juvenile detention center. Jasmine saw herself as street savvy and was connected to the "streets" both by virtue of her personal history and through her boyfriend and others in her social circle. Her boyfriend and friendship circle outside of class constituted relational resources in support of a street-savvy identity. Like Connie, Jasmine also encountered physical and verbal altercations from other girls whom she perceived to be jealous of her relationship.

On a ride to lunch from school with a researcher, Jasmine pointed out her high-rise apartment building and said: "This is the ghetto. It might not look like the ghetto where you're from, but it is. . . . If you weren't from those apartments and you didn't know anyone around there, you might get beat up or robbed while you walked through." She says, however, that the complex was safer now because the trouble-makers were all dead or in jail. Living in this complex, which had a history of violence, was a material resource in support of Jasmine's street-savvy identity.

At school Jasmine was single-mindedly focused on her academic work, but outside of school, conversations with her friends drifted to events and people in the local neighborhood, most of whom she reported had dropped out of school. In one observation, Jasmine was discussing a local shooting that had occurred over the Thanksgiving break. When asked whether she knew the gunman, Jasmine laughed and answered, "Yeah I know him, but when the police come around I don't." In another conversation, Jasmine expressed resentment at being compared to another student who was also pregnant but whom she perceived as not having had to face the same kinds of difficulties in life: "Me and Holly have two different situations. First of all my momma don't buy me [designer jeans and sneakers]. . . . I been on my own since I was twelve. Don't nobody give me nothin'."

On several occasions, Jasmine's conversation with her friends centered on recent fights at school or in the neighborhood—who fought whom, who won, who got "jumped," and so on. She reported that there were a lot of fights at Jackson, mostly between girls. She said that she and her friends had recorded three fights that year so far. The prevalence of these fights at school was a material resource in support of the street-savvy identity. Furthermore, her friends' preoccupation with the fights was a relational resource.

Like Victor, Jasmine held a critical perspective on her lack of access to resources in her neighborhood and at Jackson. In a discussion that occurred when Jasmine and six other Jackson students were on a visit to a local university campus, Jasmine tearfully acknowledged that she likely would never have access to such a beautiful and well-resourced campus and that being there made her feel frustrated and angry about the paucity of resources in her school and community.

Because of her poor academic history, Jasmine, like Victor, had a foot in both academic tracks at Jackson High. As already mentioned, her closest mentors at school were not teachers of academic subjects, but were the attendance clerk and a study skills teacher. Though by her senior year she was enrolled in a couple of AP courses (a material resource), she did not see the students or teachers there as central to her social circle. Jasmine characterized the school thus, as recorded in field notes:

> Jasmine begins by saying that she arrives at school at the last bell everyday to avoid the crowds of people and strong aromas of marijuana that fill the second floor hallway near her math class, which creep down from the third floor. . . . She says it has been tough being the student that applies herself to her work because she gets ostracized from her peers. She would go to the library after 3:00 as a safe haven from her misery to complete her work before track practice. Before Ms. Shelton took her under her wing (in her senior year) there were not really any other teachers on campus to whom she could relate.

This sense of Jasmine being a strong student, yet maintaining a position of independence and defining her social world outside of school, was evident in observations of Jasmine in class. Although she consistently did her work, and scolded classmates when they arrived late or were disruptive, Jasmine was also quite critical of her teachers and the instruction she experienced and was not afraid to express her strong opinions to her teachers directly. One morning, Jasmine left math class near the beginning of the class period and did not return until the first bell to change classes had rung. When she returned, her teacher asked her where she had been, and Jasmine responded that she went to get help with the math problems because he wouldn't help her. The teacher was visibly upset. Upon leaving the classroom Jasmine said that she did not like the teacher because he did not know how to teach and that the school in general was disorganized. This interaction is complex with respect to identity resources. On one hand, Jasmine assesses the teacher as not working hard enough to help her understand—in which case, she might view this incident as evidence of the ways that the material resources do not support her learning, or her academic identity. Yet, she clearly draws on the ideational resource that she can be proactive and in charge of her schooling to foster her push to find help elsewhere in the school.

THESE PROFILES of Jasmine and Victor illustrate the fluidity and variation in the categories of African American racial identity that we have identified. These students' stories also reinforce the point that these identities not only relate to students' experiences at school and the opportunities that are afforded to them in that context, but also to the identity possibilities they take up and challenge both locally and from the broader society. Both Jasmine and Victor had some (but not full) access to opportunities for participation in academics, and had some access to material and relational resources for practice-lined identities in school. They held critical social views yet did not share the sense of hope and personal responsibility for social change that Alonzo and Adrienne did— both ideational resources. For Victor, this took the form of critique and embracing a connection to the African American community. Jasmine understood how racial lines and social stratification imposed limitations on her, but she also remained deeply connected to her street-savvy girl-friend-of-a-gangster identity. In some ways, both of these students wrestled with the media-supported African American identity (an ideational resource) that positions black students as "hard" criminals and gangsters.

Victor wrestled with this because he worried that it aligned with what others expected of him, and Jasmine struggled in a similar way, finding status in her affiliation with a boyfriend who embodied this stereotype.

Conflicting Identities in Sports: Gozi

Taken together, Chapters 2 and 4 could leave one with the impression that out-of-school settings are unproblematic for the construction of learning identities, while schools are fraught with difficulties for students' establishing academic or learning identities. However, students who held conflicting identities existed in out-of-school learning settings as well. Gozi was one such student in track.

The students discussed in Chapter 2 found identities as learners in track readily available. Not so for Gozi. He was tall—about 6 feet—and thin, with dark brown skin and hair shaved very close to his head. He was unsure of himself and spoke softly, often mumbling. In practice, he was playful and sometimes off-task, and as the season progressed he was often singled out by the coach as goofing off or not paying attention, even when he was paying attention. He ran the 200-meter event, but wanted to run hurdles or the 100-meter race. Like many of the male track athletes, track was not Gozi's first sport; he had both played basketball and run track since his freshman year. Gozi was enrolled in an advanced college preparatory curriculum, but his grades ranged from B's in most things to C's and even an occasional D in math and science.

Gozi considered basketball to be his primary sport. By his junior year, however, it was evident that he was not going to be a star on the basketball team. According to him, the basketball coach did not give him enough playing time during the games to showcase his skill because of the presence of the younger brother of a professional basketball player who was also on the team. At this time, he began to think about taking track more seriously. In many ways, then, this change of heart could have led to Gozi being on an identity trajectory that centrally included track. And yet, as the season progressed, Gozi's participation remained marginal. By the end of the season, he had virtually stopped being involved with the team.

One reason that he did not develop a strong identity in track had to do with his relationship with his track coach, Coach J. When interviewed, both Gozi and Coach J talked about an incident that occurred when Gozi was a freshman, and both portrayed this moment as one that laid the foundation for their contentious relationship. Once, when the track team was practicing, running long distances for conditioning, Gozi and another student caught the bus part of the way (and pretended they had made the full run) rather than running the entire course. From Coach J's perspective, this was an indication of Gozi being both lazy and a goof-off, while for Gozi, this was simply a mistake he had made at the misdirection of an older teammate. The poor relationship with Coach J created a paucity of relational resources for Gozi, which led to a shortage of material and ideational resources overall.

This history, as well as Gozi's tendency to be a bit distracted in practice, resulted in Coach J not expecting much of Gozi, thus virtually ignoring him during practices, except to be punitive when he perceived Gozi to be goofing off. In our interviews with Coach J, whenever he talked about Gozi, he gave examples of times when Gozi was not doing what he was supposed to be doing, though there were lots of moments during practice and track meets when Gozi tried his best. For instance, he described one incident where another coach reported to him that Gozi was riding a bike around the track. Coach J reported that he told Gozi to get off the bicycle, then gave him extra drills. Coach J gave Gozi a goal to reach during these drills (he had to finish in less than a certain number of seconds), and he purposely made the goal almost impossible for Gozi to reach. The punitive relationship between Coach J and Gozi resulted in Gozi receiving less guidance and support than many of the other athletes, which did not help his performance and which then led to further disinvestment in him on the part of Coach J. In an interview midseason, Gozi wistfully acknowledged that he was not one of Coach J's "favorites."

Gozi's being unsure about whether he preferred basketball or track also affected their relationship. As a freshman and sophomore Gozi put more time and energy into basketball, which Coach J thought was a bad decision. On one occasion Coach J told one of the researchers that Gozi wanted to pursue basketball even though he averaged "like two points per game!" By the time Gozi decided he was serious about track, Coach J had already written him off. Gozi also did not make strong connections with the other track athletes, in part because of the way he was marginalized by Coach J. Eventually, Gozi gave up on finding a place in track and ended the season unsure about whether or not he would return the following season.

Gozi's relationship with the coach also affected his access to material resources. Gozi reported that he wanted to run the 100-meter sprint, yet Coach J kept him in the 200- and 400-meter races. His times did not significantly improve over the course of the season, and he did not learn to interact with new equipment or in new events in meaningful ways.

The poor relationship with Coach J also mattered for Gozi's access to ideational resources. Coach J saw him as a lazy goof-off who didn't really want to work—thus Gozi rarely received the kind of rich feedback on his performances or on thinking or feeling like a track athlete that other athletes experienced. Gozi was rarely mentored during practice and was rarely spoken to by Coach J during meets.

It can be seen that in out-of-school practices, too, young people were differentially given access to identities as full and competent participants. For Gozi, access to the material, ideational, and relational resources was not made readily available, and thus his identity as a track athlete and his level of participation and learning remained marginal.

Conclusion

For all three of the students discussed in this chapter, there existed sometimes conflicting, sometimes overlapping relational, ideational, and material resources for identity. Victor had access to relational, material, and ideational resources with respect to school, but these resources were greatly diminished once he failed the AP history course in the fall of his senior year. Victor also interpreted and responded to the shortage of learning resources at Jackson High in ways that contributed to his diminishing school-oriented identity. Finally, he also struggled with an ideational resource that indicated that he should be "hard."

Jasmine, too, had access to resources for her strong school-oriented identity, but also for her street-savvy identity. In fact, she had relational, material, and ideational resources in support of each of these identities, thus creating a sense of herself as *both* school oriented and street savvy. Jasmine also acted with tremendous agency to maximize the learning resources she found at Jackson, strengthening her academic identity.

Gozi, by virtue of his negative relationship with the coach, had relatively little access to relational, material, or ideational resources in track. Yet he maintained a sense of himself as having potential in the sport.

What can we learn about identity and learning from these profiles of young people who simultaneously took up seemingly incongruent identities? First, these profiles illustrate the multiple ways that society and learning settings often offer conflicting messages simultaneously. This was perhaps most evident for Jasmine, who faced strong messages both about her strengths as a student and about her affiliations with street life. Victor to a lesser degree found himself wrestling with conflicting messages about his identity and about his future.

Second, these stories show that interpreting these messages can be complex social work. All of the students struggled to figure out ways to reconcile their desires and sense of their identity with what others (and the learning settings) seemed to expect of them. Gozi faced a lack of identity resources in track, even when he saw track as a central part of his possible identity and future; ultimately, this lack of identity resources left him a marginal participant and thus weakened his identity in track. Victor, too, was greatly affected by diminishing identity resources with respect to a school identity, even though he actively participated in this decline. He found the shift in access to identity resources both puzzling and stressful. Creating a self in the face of a paucity of identity resources in a setting is difficult and perhaps near-impossible work.

Our society produces conflicting messages about what it means to be African American, but students can embrace conflicting messages. Jasmine and Victor both embraced *simultaneously* conflicting messages about what it means to be African American, drawing on the kinds of stereotypes that students articulated in Chapter 3 and on other nonstereotypical identities.

Finally, it is noteworthy that while none of these cases was about learning specific academic content, learning and access to learning resources came to play a central role in each of them. All three of the students faced a lack of learning resources in their settings. Both Victor and

Gozi responded to that paucity of learning resources by retreating and redefining themselves as less than competent participants. Jasmine, on the other hand, responded to the paucity of learning resources by working hard to garner the learning resources that she needed. In part, her ideational resources were so strong that this allowed her to reframe the lack of material resources. These differences between students underscore the fact that outcomes are determined both by the kinds of resources that are made available in the learning setting and by how one takes up and makes sense of those resources.

Attending to the material, relational, and ideational resources that are made available to young people in learning settings may also support an understanding of the ways that stereotypes can come to inform the identities of targeted students. Stereotypes can be viewed as ideational resources that become available to young people as they construct their own understanding of what it means to be African American. Indeed, the street-savvy version of student identity is quite similar to the stereotypes about African American students that young people articulated in Chapter 3 and is consistent with the research literature on stereotypes about African Americans. We can conceptualize these stereotypes, then, as an ideational resource—one that is quite prevalent and available in and through many media in our society.

Chapters 2, 3, 4, and 5 have provided a range of perspectives and insights into how African American students negotiate identities in school and in out-of-school settings. In Chapter 6, I synthesize what we have learned in these chapters.

6

Reflections on Identity and Learning

IN THE INTRODUCTION, I outlined several questions that guided the focus of this book. At the heart of these questions was how to understand the connections between identity, learning, and race for African American students. What does it mean to be an African American student in the twenty-first century when being African American is one thing and being a learner is another? How are African American youth thinking about themselves as African Americans and as students? How do learning settings (both in school and out of school) make certain configurations of identity available for students? In this chapter I synthesize what we have learned in the previous chapters and in doing so address the guiding questions posed at the beginning of this book.

How can we understand the relation between processes of learning and processes of identity? How are identities and learning related for African American students as they take part in school and/or community-based learning settings?

I have argued throughout this book that learning and engagement in learning settings are inextricably linked to students' developing identities. Conceptually, learning and identity are distinct, and I have defined these concepts in ways that make that distinction evident. I have defined learning as shifts in sense-making, performance, or the use of tools in problem-solving. In other words, learning is a concrete change in what one knows or can do. I have defined identity as a state of being that occurs when participation in a practice, whether an activity outside of school or within school, is an integral part of who one is and becomes. That is, when one comes to see the definition of who one is in relation to participation in a learning setting, one *sees oneself* as, for instance, a student, a math learner, a basketball player, or a hurdler. Thus, academic identity emerges when one feels that doing well in school is an important part of oneself. Racialized identity emerges when one sees one's membership in a racial/ethnic group as an important aspect of who one is; racialized identity can take various forms depending on how the meaning of this membership is defined.

In learning settings, both in and out of school, processes of learning and identity inform one another in multiple ways. This was evident in the descriptions of youth engaging in learning contexts such as basketball, dominoes, and track. In Chapter 2, findings showed that in these learning settings, the ways in which youth learned to play dominoes, to play basketball, and to run supported their identities as practitioners of these activities. In basketball, players talked explicitly about the connection between their *learning* key aspects of the sport and *becoming* basketball players, and that becoming was a part of youths' future vision for themselves. In dominoes, the novice player David was able to move from having very little knowledge of the game to having much more knowledge of the game in ways that built up his identity as a competent domino player. Importantly, for David his current lack of knowledge never challenged the notion that he *could be* a successful domino player. Similarly, in track, even athletes who began the sport with very little motivation, such as Octavia (whose mother pressured her to join the team), were able to gain the expertise to participate in their sport competently. Octavia came to see herself as having both a social and athletic role on the track team. In all these examples, learning and identity processes supported one another, whereby learning strengthened youths' identities in these practices, while their developing identities supported their desire to continue to learn. There were also counterexamples to this process in out-of-school settings, however. Chapter 5 showed the track athlete Gozi caught in a negative learning and identity cycle, where he was not able to gain access to new knowledge and skills and thus disinvested in a track identity over time.

In school settings, there was also evidence of this link between learning and identity processes. In Chapter 4, Alonzo and Adrienne both had very strong student identities, which were supported by the ways that promoted their engagement in learning and schooling. They participated in learning activities in the classroom fully, and that participation supported their identities as students on a successful academic trajectory. Conversely, Claude and Connie failed to develop strong identities as students; they did not have access to (nor did they take up) resources for learning at school. In Chapter 5, both Victor and Jasmine took up complex and conflicting identities, and their opportunities for learning and engaging in the academic setting mirrored these identities: at times these students had access to learning resources, but at other times they perceived a lack of access to resources for learning.

Just as Gozi disengaged from a track identity, Victor disengaged from a student identity over time, in part because of an experience of failure in the classroom that had both concrete and ideological consequences for his identity. Jasmine maintained both a strong student identity and a strong street-savvy identity and tried to separate her sense of who she was in school from a sense of who she was outside of school. Both her student identity and her street-savvy identity were supported by access to resources for learning and peer interactions at Jackson High, which included some college preparatory classes and a peer group that was also street savvy.

Both Jasmine's and Victor's stories raise the issue of the necessity of understanding identity and learning as *trajectories* rather than as fixed traits in time. Identities and participation in practices are never static, and it is critical that studies of identity recognize its fluid nature over time. These trajectories are shaped by multiple moment-to-moment interactions as youth go about their daily lives. In other words, micro-interactions in learning moments come to shape broader trajectories of learning and identity. This is a critical point to understand for teachers and others who work with young people because it means that the bulk of what students will take from learning environments is the accumulation of multiple small-scale interactions where students are given access to learning or not, where their identities as learners are afforded or constrained.

Another important point raised by understanding learning and identities as trajectories rather than as static traits is that one's perception of the trajectory one is on works to shape that trajectory through the way it influences one's participation in the learning setting. This was perhaps most evident with Victor and Jasmine. Victor began high school on a learning and identity trajectory toward college; but when he experienced failure in the AP history class, his perception of himself changed, and he began to engage with the learning settings of the classroom quite differently. He no longer believed that college was right for him, and his engagement in classroom activities lessened, while his critique of the paucity of learning resources available to him intensified. In other words, when his view of his identity trajectory shifted, so too did the nature of his participation in the learning settings connected to that trajectory.

How do learning settings make identities available to students, and how are certain identities made available and not others?

Much of the analysis in these pages has been geared toward understanding not only the types of identities that students were constructing, but also how these identities were afforded and/or constrained by the contexts in which the students participated. A main tenet of this book has been that both learning and identities are fostered in relation to one another as youth take part in culturally and socially organized learning activities in school and communities. In other words, youths' identities are not constructed out of thin air; rather, they are fostered (purposefully or incidentally) by the organization of learning settings, the roles youth are accorded and take up in those settings, the opportunities for relationship-building with others, and access to valued knowledge—in short, by the opportunities for learning and for connection that are *offered* in learning settings.

Access to Learning Resources

Throughout this book, I have highlighted several important aspects of this learning and identity-offering process. With respect to learning, identifying access to learning resources is rather obvious, particularly in out-of-school practices. In the examples I have highlighted throughout, several critical processes made learning available to young people in learning settings in and out of school. These include (1) the presence of scaffolding and support for learning challenging content, (2) in-the-moment evaluation and feedback, and (3) access to the knowledge that one needs to become a competent participant or expert in a domain.

Scaffolding and Support for Learning   The out-of-school settings were strong models of how learning settings can provide appropriate scaffolding such that novices can participate competently in the practice and participate in ways that support their learning. This was evident in dominoes when David had access to help when he was unsure about how to make a play. Furthermore, over the course of several turns, he was able to use that help as modeling for how to make an appropriate play without having to admit that he didn't know what to do. Similarly, in dominoes at the adult level, a structure was built into the play of the game such that more expert players chided, encouraged, and offered hints to less expert players. Thus, just engaging in play involved encountering scaffolding to more sophisticated levels of play.

In Victor's case, his history and chemistry class settings failed to offer such scaffolding, to the extent that Victor could not cognitively engage the lessons and eventually gave up trying. In the AP history class, Victor found it challenging to perform at the level of the other students in the class, especially because he started the class late in the semester. While there are no detailed data on his participation in this class, by his report Victor could not find ways to engage the academic material, given that he was behind the other students in the class. So the structures Victor needed for success were not in place in his classes.

Evaluation and Feedback   Structures that supported immediate evaluation and feedback were characteristic of the out-of-school learning settings. In basketball, for example, players received feedback constantly as they engaged in the drills and scrimmage activities during practice and as they executed plays and defenses during games. This evaluation and feedback came from both coaches and peers and conveyed the message that the goal of play was both to win and to get better; getting better was, in fact, in the service of winning. Similarly, in track, the coach offered verbal feedback as he critiqued the players' performances, visual feedback as he showed them how they should be moving differently, and other feedback with respect to what they should be hearing as they listened to the sound their feet made on the track as they ran. In dominoes, which is a less formal practice, players received feedback in the form of teasing in the moments of game play, but also in the form of a post-hoc analysis of game play after a hand was over. Both formative and summative feedback were offered through these processes.

In the school settings, such feedback was much less available to students, especially with respect to the content they were learning and the extent to which they understood this content. For Victor, the feedback came in the form of failure in the history class—not doing well on class assignments, knowing that he was not understanding, and ultimately receiving an F in the class. It didn't seem that Victor found this feedback useful to his learning, as he was unable (or unwilling) to take such feedback and use it to learn the content of the course. He seemed to take up only that he was failing—not particular aspects of the curriculum that he could understand and draw on in more powerful ways.

Similarly, Claude and Connie received feedback in the form of grades, but this feedback did not seem to be as central to their lives, in part because they were so disconnected from the domain of school. Also at play here may have been the paucity of feedback with respect to what they understood about the content in their courses. In this way, the school settings seem to have separated feedback from learning; feedback became an evaluation with evaluation as its endpoint, rather than evaluation with supporting learning as its endpoint. It is also likely that Connie's and Claude's poor attendance rates additionally hampered their lack of access to responsive feedback about learning.

However, recall that there were students who had less access to responsive feedback in out-of-school settings. For instance, Gozi received little feedback on his track performances and even less response on how he could improve. He was most often ignored and when he did receive feedback, it was negative criticism. He thus received much less feedback than many of his teammates.

Access to the Domain   In Chapter 2, I made the argument that the out-of-school learning settings that I studied made access to the important knowledge in the domain available to young people. In part, this is closely related to the issues of scaffolding and feedback because it is through these processes that youth gain access to acquiring the skills and knowledge that the field views as important. In track, basketball, and dominoes, participants were routinely offered access to the types of skills and knowledge that these activities valued and that would ultimately result in the development of expertise in the domain. In dominoes this meant that players learned to make more and more expert plays and that learning occurred as a normal part of their play. In track and basketball, it meant that practice sessions were structured in ways that supported students in building up the skills and knowledge that expert play required.

This access was a bit more complicated in school settings. At Jackson High, Adrienne and Alonzo were afforded a certain amount of access to content learning in their classes, especially as compared with students who were not in the AP track. However, in a moment when access was less available (such as in the class where Adrienne's teacher showed movies instead of teaching music theory), Adrienne sought out access to learning by attending other classes in which she was not enrolled. Similarly, Jasmine was enrolled in classes where her access to domain knowledge was variable, but she interacted with these contexts in ways that increased that access. For instance, when she felt that her math teacher was not helping her understand a set of mathematics problems, she left the classroom and went to another teacher for help. She also advocated for increased access to learning resources in the domain when she encouraged teachers to focus on teaching content, rather than managing other students' behavior. Thus, both Adrienne and Jasmine acted in ways that increased their access to domain knowledge.

Access to Identity Resources

Besides identifying how learning settings can make resources for learning more or less available to students, the previous chapters have also examined how learning settings made resources for identity available to students. There is some overlap here. Since learning supports identity, obviously when students have access to learning resources, they also have access to identity resources. Still, there were ways that learning settings supported identities more specifically. These included (1) allowing learners to put something of themselves into the practice, including taking up specific roles, (2) access to material resources for identity, (3) access to relational resources for identity, and (4) access to ideational resources for identity.

Putting Something of Oneself into the Practice   In Chapter 2, I noted several ways that out-of-school learning settings encouraged young people to put something of themselves into the practices of basketball, dominoes, and track. In track and basketball, athletes took up both the formal roles that were assigned to them (as point guards or hurdlers, for example) and the informal roles that they saw as being uniquely aligned with their personal strengths and proclivities. For instance, one track athlete identified herself as the "mama" of the team because she took care of others; a basketball player saw himself as the motivator because he kept his teammates' spirits up during difficult games and practices. In dominoes, and in adult play especially, the game became a forum for conversations about manhood and social life, such that the elder players used the game as a space to teach life lessons to the younger players. In all of these practices, participants engaged in uniquely African American language forms and communication styles, including speaking AAVE, boasting, teasing, and signifying.

In the school settings, students had some opportunities to put something of themselves into the school and classroom. Alonzo, Adrienne, and Jasmine took up these opportunities in various ways. Adrienne and Jasmine sought out learning opportunities, and Jasmine demanded that she be taught; these are two instances of students inserting their needs and desires into school learning settings. Alonzo's senior project is another example of how students found spaces to enact aspects of themselves at school. He chose to do a senior project on African American leaders and subsequently created a project that connected to an important aspect of who he is and to his heritage. However, students in schools did not discuss their particular roles in the classroom, nor did they talk about schools and classrooms as places where they could express themselves or have aspects of who they were taken up and valued—though perhaps Alonzo accomplished this through his leadership activities and Adrienne did so through cheerleading.

Material Resources   Material resources, explored in Chapter 5, refer to the physical artifacts in a setting—that is, ways that the physical environment, its organization, and the artifacts in it support one's sense of connection to the practice. Material resources in school include things such as the desks, backpacks, and pencils in addition to other tangible resources that influence students' ability to connect with the setting and see themselves as students. For instance, the Spanish teacher who did not speak Spanish illustrates a lack of material resources for students for both learning and identity development (and as learners of Spanish more specifically). Jackson High posed a challenge with respect to material resources for identities of students in myriad ways, including poorly equipped classrooms, science classes without lab material, and teacher and student absenteeism. In other ways, however, Jackson did provide material resources that supported student identity, including the existence of classrooms, lessons, and assignments and access for some to AP courses and other enrichment and extracurricular activities (for instance, cheerleading and a youth digital music program). These resources created opportunities for students to learn and offered them forms of participation in activities associated with identities as students.

In settings outside of school, material resources included the track itself, the gym and weight room facilities, and uniforms. Additional resources included access to learning how to use specialized equipment associated with the practice, such as the starting blocks and hurdles in track, the basketball and hoop in basketball, and the tiles and scorecard in dominoes.

Relational Resources   Relational resources for identity development involve interpersonal connections to others and speak to how positive relationships with others can increase connection to the practice. In Chapter 2, the track coach supported relational resources for members of the girls' relay team when he engaged the runners in conversation around their future careers and offered a business idea wherein members of the team could work together in these careers. In dominoes, relational resources included conversations that occurred during play that supported connection and friendship among players. In the case of Gozi (Chapter 5), lacking connection (or rather, having a negative connection) with the track coach resulted in a diminishment of identity resources for him in track.

Contrary to instances in which individuals struggled to navigate them, relational resources were readily available at Jackson High. This was evident for Alonzo, who had a strong peer network of similarly academically successful African American males who also had strong identities as students. Jasmine, too, had access to a wide network of personal support, which included the attendance clerk who brought her fruit in the morning, the staff member who invited Jasmine to live with her after she became pregnant, and Ms. Shelton, who mentored Jasmine. Claude and Connie also felt a strong sense of personal connection at Jackson, though that connection was mainly to their street-savvy peer group. However, both Claude and Connie were also familiar with administrators and had teachers who tried to intervene to support their academic trajectories. Noteworthy, then, is the fact that the *types* of relational resources are important for understanding identities in school settings. In other words, it may not be enough to just have relational resources to support a school or academic identity— students must also have access to significant learning resources, or connections to others must involve *learning*. Likewise, connections to others in a school alone may not be enough to support an academic identity, or perhaps more precisely, the racialized identities made available in the school setting could be antithetical to the development of an academic identity.

Ideational Resources   Ideational resources refer to ideas about oneself and one's relationship to and place in the practice and the world; these ideas also involve what is valued and what is good. In some ways, ideational resources are subjective, in that two students could take very different ideational resources from the same setting. Consider Alonzo and his peer group, for example. Teachers, staff, and administrators all positioned Alonzo as college bound. So who he was in the setting was an ideational resource, in that Alonzo was able to draw on this ideal positioning to construct his student identity, as well as to garner learning resources at Jackson High. Victor, to some degree, had access to some of the same ideational resources early in his high school career, but a key event (his failure in AP history) caused him to reinterpret this sense of who he was in the setting and shift his academic trajectory.

In out-of-school settings, ideational resources included viewing oneself as a future participant of the practice and as a competent contributor to the team or group. This sense of participants as being competent and on trajectories to future competence was readily made available by others in the setting through declarations such as "You're gonna be a hurdler." There is also evidence of this in students' own words, such as the basketball player who talked about the kind of player he planned to become in the following year.

Prevalent ideas about the available racialized identity could also be conceptualized as an ideational resource. That is, stereotypes that define how others tend to view African Americans come to be an ideational resource that affects identity development, as seen in Chapters 3, 4, and 5. African American students conveyed multiple definitions of what it meant to be African American. These ways students have to make sense of the world become the "stuff" from which identities are constructed. Victor, for example, was clearly hamstrung by a version of what he felt it meant to others for him to be African American.

What role do racialized identities play in engagement in school learning settings for African American students, and how can we conceptualize these racialized identities in ways that are not oversimplified or essentialized?

I have said very little thus far about where racialized identities fit into all of this. The two questions above, like the questions about identity and learning, have both a theoretical component and a practical one. Theoretically, I am concerned with how we conceptualize, think about, and write about African American racialized identities. We cannot assume that there is one version of African American identity, which people have more or less of; we must assume heterogeneity. Yet, constructs of race and ethnicity can be a "container of coherence"; that is, they are one way that we can divide up the world and explain some things with those divisions (McDermott and Varenne, 1995). My colleague Carol Lee once said of teaching African American students, "Knowing the ethnicity of the students in front of you doesn't tell you everything about those students, but it does tell you something" (personal communication). Similarly, sociologist Fred Erickson has noted, "100 percent of Mexicans don't hit piñatas 100 percent of the time" (personal communication). What Lee and Erickson both express with these statements is the tension of studying race and racialized identity: the categories that we use to understand students and their backgrounds are both powerful and limited.

Practically, I am concerned with understanding how racialized identities, and sense-making about race, are related to academic identity and the development of one's sense of place in and connection to school. Clearly, this interaction among race, learning, and schooling will take shape in different ways in different learning settings. Thus, an important aspect of this work is to explore how *particular* learning settings give rise to *particular* identities. The data presented in this book speak to both these theoretical and practical questions in a variety of ways.

Range in African American Identities

Racialized identities are complex, informed by a wide range of factors from multiple levels of analysis (including individual, interpersonal, institutional, and societal), and tremendously heterogeneous within groups. Chapters 3, 4, and 5 all speak to this heterogeneity. In Chapter 3, student interviews highlighted the variations in the nature of African American identities. These data revealed that students felt race mattered in some ways and did not matter in others; and they interpreted being African American as involving collective struggle, being faced with shared inequities, and having to manage the negative stereotypes others have about African Americans.

Chapter 4 offered two contrasting versions of African American identities: school oriented and socially conscious, and street savvy. Students with school-oriented and socially conscious identities defined their African American identity as involving giving back to their communities and saw themselves as part of a long line of African American historical figures who worked for the betterment of their communities. Both Alonzo and Adrienne fit into this category, and both took as central their commitment to personal and academic success as well as the betterment of their community. They viewed their blackness as part and parcel of their commitment to schooling and academic success and did not view their academic success as "selling out" or "acting white." The street-savvy identity was embodied by Claude and Connie and was in some ways a default African American identity that viewed blackness as being "hard" or "gangster." This mirrors longstanding stereotypes in the United States about African Americans as criminals.

The portrayals of Victor and Jasmine in Chapter 5 added complexity and nuance to the discussion of racialized and academic identities. Both of these students embraced some aspects of the school-oriented and socially conscious identity and some aspects of the street-savvy identity. Victor held the socially conscious version of African American identity that involved a heightened sense of the responsibility African Americans have to be accountable to their communities, and a sense that he was part of a long legacy of proactive black activists and historical figures. Initially, he also viewed himself as being school oriented. But during his senior year, he began to doubt his future as a college student and expressed concern about the tension between the street-savvy version of African American identity that he thought others expected of him and the socially conscious version toward which he was inclined.

Jasmine, in contrast, had a long history of embracing a street-savvy version of African American identity, which for her involved illegal activity and poor school achievement. However, as she progressed through high school, she purposefully decided to take up a school-oriented identity while in school, yet still maintained her street-savvy identity outside of school. Ultimately, her becoming pregnant by her street-savvy boyfriend played a role in shifting her academic goal from attending Princeton University to attending the local community college, and that resulted in a long-term absence from school.

Relation between African American Identities and School

Race and racialized identities interact with learning identities in important ways. Claude and Alonzo were very different kinds of students, and they defined their African American identity in contrasting ways—one as a thug and the other as part of an historical legacy of achievement.

One of the core points of Chapter 4 was that these racialized identities, like learning and academic identities, were made available by our society writ large but also by particular interactions and resources in proximal learning settings. In other words, the categories of racialized identity provided by our society are filtered in important ways and made available to youth through local institutions and settings (such as schools, churches, and community centers). At Jackson High, students were offered racialized identities as part of a particular version of academic identities, and those racialized and academic identities informed one another.

In Chapters 3, 4, and 5, I suggested that particular kinds of African American racialized identities better support identities as students. For Alonzo and Adrienne, the school-oriented and socially conscious African American identity supported high achievement in school, which then confirmed and strengthened their academic identities. Similarly, Claude's and Connie's street-savvy identity did not support achievement in school and thus weakened their potential identities as students. Victor and Jasmine each took up some aspects of a street-savvy identity, which in the end seemed to have had some negative consequences on their schooling outcomes.

Access to these forms of identity within the school context was quite powerful for students, but students also acted on these environments in critical ways to garner or resist available resources. For instance, Jasmine was proactive in garnering resources for both learning and academic identity, while Victor seemed less able or willing to actively seek out such resources. Instead, he resisted a school context that he felt didn't serve him well.

Chapter 3 focused on stereotypes in particular and presented data on how students understood what it meant to be African American. These students reinforced two main themes of African American identity: first, that others assume that all African Americans are thugs or gangsters, as well as poor students, and second, that being African American involves a collective struggle in the face of inequities. The focus on stereotypes, and the prevalence of the negative stereotypes of African Americans as thugs and bad students, mirrored Victor's assertion in Chapter 1 that others expected him to portray a "hard" persona, even when such a self-presentation felt inauthentic to him. The street-savvy portrayals that

Claude and Connie took up also reified this version of what it means to be African American.

The seemingly unreflective process of taking up the street-savvy identity is interesting food for thought. Previously (Nasir, 2010), I have made the distinction between "authentic" identities and identity "parroting" and have argued that students like Claude, Zeus, and Connie simply take up available identities for which there are significant identity resources in both the local community and the broader society. One could argue, however, that imitation (called "mirroring" by some psychologists) is at the heart of what it means to be human; thus, all identities require resources in the immediate environment, and all identities involve some degree of imitation or mirroring (consider the development of gender identities in children around ages three and four). For the purposes of this book, it is enough, perhaps, to simply point out that identities always consist of the raw material that people find in the social contexts around them and occur in social interaction with others.

These social interactions involving identity resources occur as part of a broader cultural landscape. Recent work grounded in anthropology offers a way to describe the cultural milieu of practices and activities within which social identities are taken up. Holland et al. (1998) argue that cultural practices are "figured worlds" that carry with them a set of norms, expectations, and ideas that constrain and enable particular kinds of participation in these practices and that become shared among practice participants. Within these figured worlds, individuals both act with agency in authoring themselves and are acted upon by social others as they are positioned (as members, nonmembers, or certain kinds of members).

In addition to these positionings, students' racial identities also play an important role in the development of students' school identities and trajectories. In Chapter 7, I consider the role teachers and schools have in supporting the racial and academic identities of students. I consider the research literature on effective teachers of African American students and draw on three examples of what such identity-building teaching practices look like: an historical look at African American segregated schools in the South, a community-based youth program, and an African-centered charter school in Chicago.

7

Up You Mighty Race
Teaching as Identity-Building

THIS BOOK HAS HIGHLIGHTED the importance of racial and academic identities to students' engagement in school. The title of this chapter, "Up You Mighty Race," is a quotation from Marcus Garvey, a Black Nationalist leader and advocate for the rights of African Americans in the early twentieth century. Garvey was a believer in bringing together members of the African American community to protest their unfair treatment in the United States and to build stronger and more resilient communities. A part of his message was that African Americans should reconnect to their African homeland and reclaim identities of dignity. I use this quotation here because it illustrates this chapter's theme of purposeful identity construction.

It is perhaps controversial to argue that schools *should* engage in racial socialization and/or other identity work with students, but as illustrated, this "identity-building" is already happening in schools and classrooms—it just happens more implicitly, rather than explicitly. Research tells us very little about the degree to which or in what ways schools explicitly engage in the work of identity-building. Thus, we know, from a research perspective at least, very little about what these processes might look like if schools explicitly supported students' racialized and academic identities or engaged in purposeful racial socialization.

I focus in this chapter on exploring how teachers and administrators could consciously engaged in supporting racial socialization and academic identity work with their students. I discuss material resources, relational resources, and ideational resources in relation to three examples that offer insight into how to engage African American students purposefully in developing positive racialized and academic identities. One example stems from the literature examining African American schools before desegregation in the South, another comes from a study of an African-centered school in Chicago, and the final one comes from a study of a youth development program in California. For each, I explore the ways that these contexts make material, relational, and ideational identity resources available to students, and I discuss the ways in which these resources might help shape young people's racial and academic identities.

My aim in this chapter is to highlight places where African American educational spaces have effectively (or rather, positively) attended to issues of identity and learning for African American students. Given this agenda, it is perhaps important to acknowledge that the educational spaces described here do not represent all educational spaces of their kind; that is, not all segregated schools in the South, African American independent schools, and community-based programs operate in the same ways. Moreover, I am not arguing that these kinds of spaces *inherently* support the learning and identities of all African American students. Nor am I arguing that the learning settings I describe are perfect and without major shortcomings. To the contrary, I acknowledge that all institutions are inherently wrought with tension and conflict; all can function to empower as well as marginalize; and they can provide access for some and withhold it from others. I am, however, viewing these settings as existence proofs in that they provide some evidence that settings which are run with the explicit intention to support both the learning and identities of African American students not only exist in our society, but can offer insight into how such settings are organized and how they provide access to learning and identity resources for young people.

Supporting Racial and Academic Identities: Three Settings

Developing Identity in African American Segregated Schools

I began this book with an historical focus on the conversation about identity and education for African Americans in part to highlight the longstanding salience of the relation between learning and identity for African American students. In the early twentieth century, questions about the kinds of people schooling was preparing African Americans to be were very much in the forefront of educational studies, as African Americans struggled to create and fund educational institutions and wrestled with questions about the kind of education that African Americans deserved (Anderson, 1988; Du Bois, 1903; Newby and Tyack, 1971; Watkins, 2001). As the century progressed, and as African American schools were established, the teachers and administrators who worked in them created educational spaces that intended to support the learning and identities of African American students.

To describe the identity resources available in segregated African American schools in the South, I draw on secondary accounts of these schools and teachers, highlighting how these schools made relational, ideational, and material resources available for both racial and academic identities and relying heavily on the work of Vanessa Siddle-Walker (1996, 2000) in particular and on Michelle Foster (1997), Jerome Morris (2001), and James Anderson (1988).

It is critical to acknowledge that both contemporarily and historically, segregated educational settings serving African American students have not simply been separate; they have also been fundamentally unequal. Before the 1954 Supreme Court decision in *Brown v. Board of Education* (and indeed to this day), schools serving African American students were funded and resourced at levels significantly below schools that served white students. African American segregated schools suffered from inferior (and in some cases unsafe) facilities, overcrowding, shorter school terms, less well educated and poorly paid teachers, and a lack of basic supplies such as pencils, paper, books, and chalkboards (Anderson, 1988; Ashmore, 1954; Darling-Hammond, Williamson, and Hyler, 2008; Kluger, 1975). Furthermore, African American students routinely received used textbooks from white schools, were not provided with transportation (even when students had long commutes to black schools), and parents, teachers, and administrators had to lobby school districts for resources (Siddle-Walker, 1996). Contemporary segregated schools serving African American students similarly compare poorly to schools attended by white students (Darling-Hammond, 2010; Kozol, 2005; Oakes, 2004). Specifically, schools attended by African American students tend to have newer and less well prepared teachers, inferior facilities, and fewer advanced course offerings. Beyond this, these schools have lower graduation rates and higher dropout rates (Darling-Hammond, 2010; Kozol, 2005). This longstanding pattern of schools underserving African American students speaks to the ways that racism has been institutionalized in our school systems. However, there have been important exceptions to these patterns—both historically and contemporarily—and nuances that attention solely to the physical resources of such schools obscures. In this section, I focus on the relational, ideational, and material resources that existed in segregated southern schools. Specifically, I discuss how these resources made learning and identities as learners (including racialized identities) available to students.

Relational Resources   Relational resources for identities as students and as African Americans were abundantly available in some segregated schools in the South.[1] As described in Siddle-Walker (1996, 2000), many African American schools in the South were often at the center of communities. Teachers, administrators, and families regularly came together to support the education of their young people; and school administrators, who required teachers to visit students' homes and attend community events, purposefully fostered the centrality of the school to the community.

The close relationships students had with their teachers inside and outside the school context supported their identities as students. Identities as African Americans were similarly supported by socialization into a community led by African American teachers and administrators who were invested in the holistic development of African American youth. African Americans in positions of authority in the school setting served as important role models for students. Therefore, personal relationships with these adults likely informed how these young people thought about what it meant to be African American. That is, interactions with African American teachers and administrators were opportunities for racial socialization.

Students and teachers reported that an important feature of segregated schools in the South was the close, caring relationships between teachers and students. One teacher said of her elementary school students: "Those kids would just come and get right down on the floor and tell you their problems. . . . We were interested in that whole child" (Siddle-Walker, 1996, 123). This teacher describes a classroom setting founded upon human relationships where learning was connected to the personal issues of the learner. A similar report from a high school student supports this point: "During our study period, we would go out of the study hall and go into some teacher's room that didn't have classes at the time. They'd sit down a long time and talk to you, in general about life, how tough it was once you graduated. . . . They would always, someone would tell us, you can't get anywhere in the world, in life, unless you have a good education" (173). In both this elementary school and high school, students had opportunities to develop relationships with teachers that went beyond the curriculum.

The African American teachers whom Foster (1997) interviewed also described a segregated school setting where students felt personally supported and connected to their teachers. One teacher reported:

> The education I received in segregated schools was a good one, primarily because of the interest of the teachers, teachers who are willing to go above and beyond the job. . . . I mean they were interested in you as a human being, in your future. They went out of their way with you as a person, to give you advice, to help you, to talk about your family problems or personal problems. They were not afraid to help you. These teachers wanted you to move ahead, they believed in you, and you were able to believe in them. (Foster, 1997, 102)

This sense of relationship between students and teachers also extended to relationships between students and the principal. One student reported (Siddle-Walker, 1996) that the principal not only encouraged her to take college entrance exams but physically drove her to the exam site on the day of the test and provided her with a pencil and money to cover the exam fees. Other students shared similar stories of support from the principal, citing examples when he helped them financially so that they could stay in college, such as paying for books or providing a portion of the tuition money. Stories like these paint a picture of support from administrators who took up a parentlike role, more often in cases where parents did not have the knowledge to support their children in their college aspirations (financially or otherwise). The relational resources, then, were both about personal relationships between teachers, administrators, and students that could then inform the kinds of students, as well as the kinds of African Americans the young people became, and about the intimate ways in which these relationships linked with material resources, such as having access to a college entrance exam.

It is important to note that the relational resources that students experienced, through their caring interactions with teachers and administrators, were part of the ethic of care in the schooling institution more broadly (Noddings, 1992). Siddle-Walker (1996) calls such caring and personal relationships in segregated southern schools "institutional caring." She writes, "This caring encompassed both the human relationships that existed between the major participants and the institutional structures created as a result of that caring" (201). One instance of the way caring was built into the institutional practices of the school was the structure of homeroom, whereby one teacher served as the homeroom teacher and mentor for a student for his or her entire four years of high school. One teacher said of this practice: "You get to know the student well. You had to accept and love them" (125). Similarly, a student reported: "It was like a group of teachers had a lot of concern and care and looked out after us for those four years. And it became like a family. They were like a family to us" (125). In other words, attention to the personal aspect of schooling was built into the norms and structures of the school, and the student experienced caring from multiple sources in the school environment.

The sense of personal connection and belonging to a community was also evident in relationships cited between parents and school personnel. Communication between parents and teachers was facilitated by the multiple opportunities for informal conversation about students that occurred during school events and activities, since the principal required teachers to attend Parent-Teacher Association meetings and other school events. Additionally, parental attendance was also strong because in small southern communities, school events were places where the black community congregated. Parents' access to their child's teacher was further supported by the practice of teachers visiting students' homes and churches. One principal made a concerted effort to attend the churches and funerals of members of students' families; this was his way of being in the community, which led others to view him as a caring member of that community. He not only encouraged teachers to do the same, he also encouraged them to visit students at home regularly. Efforts like these created ample opportunities for parents and teachers to build informal relationships, as well as to check in formally about the progress of individual students in school.

In many African American schools before desegregation, many students had access to personal relationships with teachers and peers that supported their racialized and academic identities through modeling, socialization, and acts of caring. Schools were embedded within communities in ways that further supported the academic trajectories of students and allowed students to define themselves as being contributing members of their communities.

Ideational Resources   Central to these kinds of relationships between school personnel and students and their families were certain ideas and ways of thinking about education, race, and the abilities of students that pervaded African American schools. Identities as students were supported by the prevalence of ideas about the importance of education for social mobility and for maximizing one's contribution to the world, as well as by assumptions that students were smart and capable learners. I consider these ideas about African American learners to be ideational resources because they are fundamental ideas about schooling that become the necessary tools that students act upon in learning settings. In segregated African American schools, identities as African Americans were supported by socialization inside of schools, as teachers sought to prepare students for the harsh realities of prejudice and discrimination that awaited them outside of schools.

For instance, Siddle-Walker (1996) writes of the teachers at Caswell County Training School: "Although students lived in a world outside the school that offered negative appraisals of what they were capable of doing, the teacher functioned to counter these messages and offer new ones of hope and possibility through education" (122). She gives examples of teachers encouraging students to strive even in the face of discrimination and others who do not believe in their intellectual potential. She writes: "In actual practice, the ideas teachers and the principal held about teaching were revealed in the attitudes they assumed in interactions with children. On a broad level, they believed that the children could be anything they wanted to be. The larger American society sent deprecating messages about the Negro's value and status, but the teachers and principals within the school constructed a counter-message" (123).

This attention to expressing a purposeful counter-message was one way that school teachers and administrators addressed differences between how they wanted their students to see themselves and the way they anticipated how the outside world would see them. There were frequent discussions about careers and college, and students were encouraged to ignore the limits that others in society might place upon them. In this way, there was a strong link between support for academic identities (as students were encouraged to think of themselves as capable students) and racialized identities (as students were encouraged not to accept what were often characterized as inevitable limits that the outside world might place on them because of their race). These ideational resources contributed to racial socialization that prepared students for racial bias and defined what it meant to be African American in ways that differed from the definitions that were common in society at that time.

In one freedman's school for newly freed slaves in the late nineteenth century, similar attention was given to purposefully supporting ideas that could inform African American identities. Following are the lyrics from the song "Howard at Atlanta," which concluded academic lessons at the end of the school day and was sung together by the entire school (Morris, 2008):

> We are rising as a people, with the changes of our land
> In the cause of right and justice let us all united stand
> As we rose amid the conflict, when the battle storm was high
> With returning peace we're rising, like the eagles to the sky. (21)

These lyrics frame an identity for African Americans in relation to being members of both the nation and an oppressed group. The song defines the newly freed slaves as freedom fighters, fighting in the cause of justice in their own land and "rising as a people." The song highlights both an American identity and an African American identity, rooted in the struggle for equality.

The teachers interviewed by Foster (1997) also attended to the ways that teachers in segregated schools discussed issues of race and inequality with their students, thus supporting academic identities and academic motivation. One teacher said:

> Again, what black kids miss as a result of desegregation is the serious kinds of conversations that we were able to have in all-black schools. Black kids are not hungry now. There are some few that want to be on top, but they are not really hungry. . . . And the reason they don't hunger is because nobody tells them that they need to hunger and thirst for education. Once they went into the integrated situation, there was no one pushing them. (9)

This teacher views conversations about race and the place of schooling in one's life and in the racial struggle as a part of the experience of students in African American schools before desegregation. She argues that the loss of these conversations in schools has resulted in a lack of motivation for African American students.

Another teacher highlighted the ways that desegregation led to what she believed to be a negative self-image for African American students with respect to school:

> I think when they integrated the schools, instead of the black kids seeing themselves as people who could go in there and make progress, they got linked and then linked themselves to all the bad things that the kids were doing. I can only relate to when I was in a segregated school. You'd go to high school commencement and I could see these kids walking up there with these four-year scholarships to places like Fisk and Howard to A&T or wherever. Now when I go to a high school graduation, the only kids I see getting scholarships are the white kids. (60)

This teacher emphasizes the importance of seeing other African American students graduating and getting scholarships to college, as well as the way that students might come to internalize the negative expectations that others have of them.

What is striking in these portrayals of the ideational resources that students had access to in developing identities as African Americans and in developing identities as students is the extent to which these identities were linked. School personnel expressed to students in varied ways that they were intellectually capable of succeeding in school, despite the fact that the outside world did not think so. These forms of racial socialization (Hughes and Chen, 1997; Thornton et al., 1990) have been linked to youth developing more positive racial identities. The descriptions of the teaching and racial socialization practices in segregated African American schools might suggest that racial socialization with respect to academics may also be positively related to academic identities and persistence in school.

Material Resources   Material resources for teaching and learning in African American schools, as illustrated in historical records, were especially sparse. Several of the teachers whom Siddle-Walker interviewed spoke to the paucity of material resources as being a major impetus for the black community's support of desegregation. For example, African American students received older books and far fewer dollars per pupil than white schools in the same district (Siddle-Walker, 1996; Anderson, 1988; Morris, 2001). Students were often required to learn in classroom settings that were burning hot in the summer and freezing cold in the winter (Anderson, 1988). Practical constraints also impeded students' access to learning and identities. Kluger (1975) relates a story of a group of African American students who walked to school (because the district would not provide transportation for them) being purposely splattered with mud by a passing school bus full of white students. This story exemplifies how the paucity of resources was due to the way society viewed the worth of African Americans. Arguably, messages about worth in society were a powerful form of racial socialization; it is also plausible that the scarcity of material resources for learning negatively affected students' learning as well as their identities as learners.

Despite segregated African American schools having poor resources overall, the material resources in those schools did at times support the academic and racial identities of students. One important aspect of students' access to material resources in segregated black schools was that although resources were sparse overall, all students had access to the resources that did exist, such as books, paper, pencils, college entrance exams (and even the money for fees in some cases, as noted above). Additionally, parents were instrumental in working together to increase the kinds of resources that students had access to. For example, at one school, parents supported the school's material resources by providing furniture, labor, and books and by donating and raising money for programs and building improvements. Furthermore, at some schools students could choose from a large number of extracurricular and club activities that supported students' connection with the school, and which could be considered tangible resources that students could use in identity-building (Siddle-Walker, 1996, 100).

I do not want to downplay the impoverished nature of the access to material resources for learning present in segregated African American schools, but it is important to recognize that to some degree the kinds of relationships and caring described here supported access to learning and school resources because every student was seen as valuable and important and as having academic potential. On balance, then, though schools did attempt to create access to the material resources that did exist, material resources were still largely lacking.

The range of relational and ideational resources in some segregated schools in the South, even in the face of abysmal and strikingly unequal material resources, speaks to the power of what Holland et al. (1998) have called "figured worlds." Local settings, guided by a set of norms, practices, and beliefs, can create an alternative world where African American students have access to a sense of belonging to a school community, where they can define blackness as part of being a strong student, and where against staggering odds, they can achieve academically.

Encouraging Positive Identities in an African-Centered School

The second example of teaching for identity-building comes from the work of Lee (2009) in an independent African-centered school in Chicago. In this section I draw on her 2009 account of the history and practices of the school, as well as on my own observations from a visit to the school in 2004.

New Concept Development Center (NCDC) began as a Saturday enrichment and tutoring program in 1972 amid the Black Power movement and expanded to a full-day elementary school in 1974. This school would later evolve into three additional charter schools and comprise what is now called the Betty Shabazz International Charter School. The goal of the school was to "teach African American history and culture as well as imbue the values of Black self-love and cooperation among the children it served" (Lee, 2009, 211). The school was founded by and for members of Chicago's black community and was conceptualized as a community-based institution. The initial staff were not trained educators; rather, they were college educated and dedicated to the uplift of the African American community and saw education as a core aspect of that community work.

Relational Resources   At NCDC, relationships are at the core of the educational endeavor. Teachers often serve a year as teaching assistants to experienced teachers before they head their own classroom; this year is seen as important for their training in the pedagogies and methods of African-centered teaching, and it offers novice teachers the opportunity to develop a relationship with a mentor teacher who can then support the ongoing development of their teaching. Similar to the segregated African American schools in the South, teachers at NCDC are concerned not only with developing the intellectual potential of children, but with encouraging their physical, social, emotional, and moral development as well—that is, focusing on the whole child (Lee, 2009). Thus, teachers focus on more than just delivering material; they also push students to do their best, to embrace their culture, and to give back to their families, communities, and the world. The forms of address regularly used in the school affirm the family-like nature of the relationship between students and teachers: students refer to teachers with the title Baba or Mama (meaning father or mother in Kiswahili) and their first names. Lee writes, "This makes the public statement that teachers serve an [i]n loco parentis function for the children" (218). Adults also refer to one another with these titles.

The family-like structure of the school and the attention to the development of the whole child and the school community foster a sense of personal connection among students, teachers, parents, and administrators. This sense of belonging supports students' connections to the content of their learning and to a sense of themselves as students. It simultaneously socializes students into a certain kind of African American community (one guided by African-centered values and ideas) and gives them access to a place within that community. Similar to the segregated African American schools, the teachers at NCDC are predominantly African American, thereby also providing the students with models of academically successful African American adults. Thus, racial socialization to what it means to be black occurs as students are socialized to what it means to be African American at NCDC and as they interact with African American adults who model those racial identity meanings.[2]

Ideational Resources   The focus on developing the whole child, and not just affecting the mental life of the child, serves as an important ideational resource in support of students' racial and academic identities. As with the out-of-school settings discussed in this book, an emphasis on the whole child, and attending to the multiple domains of development, supports young people's connection to learning settings and supports their identity as members of the school community. This view of attending to the whole child embodies the idea that children are more than just empty vessels to be filled. At NCDC, teachers hold the idea that within each child is great potential, or what Lee calls "a spark of the divine." This view of children as inherently valuable and bringing forth an aspect of the divine supports the belief that "each child is capable of learning complex bodies of knowledge and problem-solving strategies" (Lee, 2009, 214).

In addition to ideas about children as inherently good, there are other underlying beliefs at NCDC about the nature of teaching in an African-centered independent school context. Lee (2009) lists ten key principles that are central to the mission of African-centered teaching:

1. The social ethics of African culture as exemplified in the social philosophy of *Maat* (balance, harmony)
2. The history of the African continent and diaspora

3. The need for political and community organizing within the African American community

4. The positive pedagogical implications of the indigenous language, AAVE

5. Child development principles that are relevant to the positive and productive growth of African American children

6. African contributions in science, mathematics, literature, the arts, and societal organization

7. Teaching techniques that are socially interactive, holistic, and positively affective

8. The need for continual personal study (and critical thinking)

9. The African principle that children are "the reward of life"

10. The African principle of reciprocity; that is, a teacher sees his or her own future symbiotically linked to the development of students (Lee, 2009, 215)

These guiding principles can be viewed as a part of the ideational resources that teachers in the school draw upon as they teach and guide their students. I contend that these principles have implications for students' access to both racial and academic identities. The majority of these principles have to do with a worldview that places the African experience at the center and has a vision of teaching that sees the reciprocal relation between student and teacher as fundamental. Thus, students' identities as African Americans are framed positively and as being connected to a rich culture and historical set of people and events. Young peoples' identities as students are supported as the school context frames learning and critical thinking as a part of becoming a contributing member of the African American community.

Material Resources   These ideational resources give rise to the nature of material resources at the NCDC, which include the teachers' choice of books, visuals, and maps and the construction of spaces, which are all chosen with an African aesthetic in mind. For example, the school and classrooms are decorated with touches of African fabric and art and pictures of African and African American people. The presence of this

African aesthetic further supports the integration of students' identities as both African Americans and students as being positively related to one another. Key here is the fact that not only are the materials present, but that students' use of these materials confirms their identities as members of the community, as scholars, and as being connected to the African diaspora.

Like the segregated schools in the South that Siddle-Walker and others have described, this portrait of NCDC (and by extension the Betty Shabazz International Charter School) illustrates that strong interpersonal relationships and narratives about what it means to be African American can subvert the common stereotypical definitions and create alternative identity spaces for African American students.

Deconstructing and Supporting Racial Identities in a Community Youth Program

The third example of how racial and academic identity can be supported in teaching comes from a community-based youth program in Oakland, California, called the Positive Minds Group (PMG); it is one of several youth development programs run by The Mentoring Center, a local nonprofit organization. PMG was founded in 1995 by three youth from the local community who had graduated from a transition program that The Mentoring Center ran inside of an incarceration facility for youth. The weekly program focused on "correcting the mentality that gives rise to destructive behavior" (organization website, 2009). This section draws on findings from Woodland et al. (2009).

Approximately twenty to thirty youth attend PMG each week. Similar to the structure of NCDC, PMG program sessions focus on a wide range of topics, including African and African American history, personal responsibility and growth, management of emotions, and spiritual development. The program is run concurrently in two separate locations: at The Mentoring Center and at a classroom in a local high school.

The facilitators draw on "relevant movies, music videos, speeches, interviews, and personal testimonies to underscore the discussion topics" (Woodland et al., 2009, 236). Since the program is ongoing, many of the attendees are longterm "PMGers," while others come to the program for only a few sessions or attend sporadically. Youth who attend include both the "highly at-risk" population that The Mentoring Center targets (for example, youth on probation or who have multiple disciplinary referrals from their schools) and youth who are high-achieving high school and college students. Participants are predominantly, but not exclusively, African American and include both young men and young women.

Relational Resources   As with the segregated schools and NCDC, supportive relationships are a core aspect of PMG. In describing the program, one attendee remarked that the reason he continued to attend was the "love, family, and community" he experienced there (Woodland et al., 2009, 238). Other students remarked that receiving invitations from another student or family member or from other members of the community was their impetus for attending the program. Youth reported that once there the sense of community with peers was a strong incentive to keep attending. The following comment from a student detailing the positive peer support he found in the program illustrates this point:

> So I come to [PMG] to interact with these people 'cause some of the people in the world I associate myself with are not aware of those types of things and concepts. . . . They will not be able to understand and we will butt heads all the time and that is abuse for both of us 'cause we will have different understandings and that will cause stress on ourselves. . . . It was a big bonding and learning experience with other people so I decided to stay and it keeps me focused. (239)

This student appreciates the way that he finds a cohort of young people at PMG who share a set of ideas and positive goals. He calls this a "bonding and learning experience," highlighting the link for him between being connected to his peers in the room and learning new ways of thinking about himself in relation to others in the world.

PMG leadership fosters a sense of group belonging in a number of ways. For example, the PMG facilitator started a virtual group for PMG attendees on Facebook (a popular social networking site) and regularly sent out inspirational messages, reminders, and invitations to PMG sessions. The Facebook group also serves as a space for attendees to communicate with one another, share pictures, and reinforce messages and ideas conveyed within the session. For example, one PMG attendee posted a note on Facebook that after his nephew had asked him about an idea that had been extensively discussed in the group, he shared some of the PMG teachings with his nephew.

In addition to feeling close to one another and being part of a peer network that shares an important set of ideas, youth also note that the adults in the program serve as caring role models and mentors. As one student says:

> I really don't see too many real male or female Black role model figures so when I come here, I come and see that dignity. Man that inspires me. Like Mama James [a staff member], she's a woman, you know? Or like Baba Johnson, Edwards, Malik [program volunteers and staff], they actual men. . . . I want to keep those images in my mind so I can know that it's true and it's something that's achievable for me. (Woodland et al., 2009, 240)

This young person highlights how he sees program staff as people to look up to, as images of mature, positive African American womanhood and manhood. The adult staff also take up pseudo-parental roles with youth, for example, regularly loaning the students small amounts of money for food or transportation, giving them rides home after every program session, inviting them to their homes for holidays, and providing impromptu advice and mentoring on a variety of subjects. As with the segregated African American schools and with the African-centered school, these connections between program leaders and student participants support racial identities by providing young people with models for what it looks like to live and embody positive, productive African American identities. With respect to academic identities, performance and engagement in school is a regular topic in PMG sessions, and youth frequently seek out the advice of program staff about their academic trajectories.

Ideational Resources   Similar to its other resources, PMG explicitly puts forth several key ideas about race, identity, and school that might become identity resources for participants. The program is constructed around three main questions: "How do I see myself?," "Who am I?," and "Why am I here?" Undergirding each question is a set of ideas that is intended to encourage young people to develop identities that they choose for themselves, rather than identities that society or peers expect of them.

With respect to the first question, "How do I see myself?," the program encourages youth to see their identities as impressionable and to understand that they can grow and change their identities and that they can make purposeful decisions about how they see themselves. Assuredly, from an ideational perspective, the changes students are expected to make in their identities are for their betterment. In which case, the portion of the program that addresses this question highlights three concepts that describe the experience of African and African American people: *Maat* (balance, harmony), *Maafa* (the African holocaust, also known as slavery), and *Sankofa* (which means a returning or going back and retrieving what was lost). In PMG, these terms are used to ground an explicit conversation with youth about what it means to be African American and the historical shifts in these meanings. The focus in this part of the program is on understanding the historical and cultural influences that affect identity choices for contemporary African American youth.

The focus of the second major component of the program, which asks youth to consider the question "Who am I?," is on understanding oneself as an emotional, psychological, and biological being and understanding the role of personal will and choice in deciding who one will be in any given situation. Conversations and lectures concentrate on working with and understanding one's emotions and instinctual reactions and coming to see oneself as having choices about how one reacts to life situations. During these conversations, the program facilitators often draw on music, movies, and other cultural artifacts to illustrate important points and to promote the engagement of youth.

The third major component of the program asks the question "Why am I here?" and focuses on helping youth discover and understand their purpose in life. It offers models of others in the African American community who have found and lived their unique purpose.

These discussions have issues of racial and academic identities at their core and engage young people in explicit consideration of their identities, with respect to both how they think about themselves as African Americans and how they think about the role of school in their lives.

Material Resources   Material resources for identity at PMG primarily consist of resources that connect young people to the PMG community. One type of material resource is the artifacts used during the sessions. The facilitator uses slides and incorporates images and music from popular youth culture to engage the young people in the sessions, but also to help them problematize, question, and analyze these taken-for-granted images and messages. This use of cultural and racialized images and music familiar to students in their lives outside of PMG conveys the message to students that PMG is a space where they belong culturally.

Another important material resource is the weekly handouts that serve as the agenda for the meetings. Often illustrated with eye-catching images from youth culture and music, these handouts describe the main ideas for the day's session. Participants take the handouts with them when they leave the session, which then ideally (and potentially) provide them with a kind of border-crossing artifact, taking ideas from PMG into other activity settings in their lives (home, school, peer networks).

PMG also offers other material resources that signal membership, build community, or support the family-like ethos of the group. For example, light snacks are provided during sessions, increasing the sense of "home" at PMG. Additionally, students can request free bus and train tickets to support their transportation to and from sessions as well as to school.

The range of material resources at PMG reinforces a sense of belonging in the space, thus supporting the kind of relational identities that I have described. Furthermore, the use of music and artifacts from youth culture contributes to the racial socialization process and conveys to young people that their culture is a welcomed part of the PMG space.

As with the segregated schools in the South and the African-centered school, PMG provides a range of relational, ideational, and material resources to support young people in feeling connected to the learning setting and in having access to African American identities and identities as learners less often found in traditional school settings.

Principles of Teaching for Identity-Building

These examples of schools and programs that practice identity-building as an important aspect of their teaching work with African

American youth have shown how alternative "figured worlds" can be constructed to provide a range of resources for African American students to develop positive racialized identities and identities as learners. I intend them only to be illustrations of practices and values that might align with teaching for the purpose of identity-building for African American youth and as support for imagining what this kind of teaching might look like in practice. To this end, important themes that cut across these three examples must be examined—themes that I believe we might view as principles that could inform a theoretical model of how schools might better support positive racialized and academic identities for African American youth. These themes are

- Caring relationships among members of the school community
- Spaces where students are cared about as whole people
- Access to material resources for all students
- Culturally relevant practices
- Explicit conversations about race and managing discrimination

Caring relationships among members of the school community. All three schools and programs supported positive, caring relationships among members of the school and learning community. Young people were viewed as competent, intellectually strong, and inherently worthy. In the segregated African American schools, students and teachers consistently alluded to spaces, formal and informal, where students could raise and discuss personal issues and struggles with their teachers. At the independent African-centered school, children and teachers were a part of a family-like community where students were highly valued and teachers were referred to as "mother" and "father" in Kiswahili. In the youth development program, young people similarly described the family-like nature of the program and their close relationships with the facilitators and other program participants.

Spaces where students are cared about as whole people. In the three examples explored, young people were cared about as people, in addition to being cared for as students or as impressionable minds. Multiple aspects of the students' development—cognitive, social, emotional, and moral—were fostered and supported. This was evident in reports of interaction between teachers and students in segregated African American schools, where teachers made time for students to talk to them about personal matters. In the African-centered school, the administration saw attending to students' whole selves as a key aspect of their mission. In the youth development program, teaching included attention to developing all aspects of the students' lives.

Access to material resources for all students. The schools and community-based program described did not have an abundance of material resources, but those they had were available to all students. In other words, the resources were not guided by a tracking or sorting system that defines some students as capable and others as less capable; instead, they were guided by a philosophy that viewed all students as having intellectual and human potential, even as carrying a divine spark for learning and promise. This valuing of all students meant that none was excluded from access to resources.

Culturally relevant practices. These schools and programs, especially the contemporary learning settings, allowed and even fostered cultural ways of communicating and being. For instance, music and videos were used extensively in PMG sessions, and students and program facilitators often used AAVE in their communication with one another. At the African-centered school, African and African American culture were represented in the practices (for example, drumming and singing at the morning circle), the physical environment (African art and fabric), and learning resources (the presence of African and African American literature). At segregated African American schools, teachers and students had conversations around shared experiences of discrimination and participated together in church and other community institutions and events.

Explicit conversations about race and managing discrimination. Finally, all three of these learning environments engaged African American young people in explicit conversations about race and managing racial discrimination. Discussions about race included both practical attention to how one might respond to discrimination and advice about how to psychologically manage being stereotyped. In each of these learning spaces, access to a myriad of resources for viewing African Americans positively undergirded teaching and learning about important historical events and historical and cultural figures in African American history.

THIS LIST is by no means exhaustive, and it overlaps in some important ways with some of the current work on culturally relevant pedagogy (Ladson-Billings, 1995), culturally responsive pedagogy (Gay, 2000), cultural modeling (Lee, 2007), and funds of knowledge (Gonzalez, Moll, and Amanti, 2005), but it could be useful in pushing forward conversations about the characteristics of schools and learning environments that fundamentally support African American students in developing both content knowledge and a positive sense of themselves as African Americans and as students. Particularly important for this discussion is how such characteristics relate to the kinds of identities (namely, as students and as African Americans) that are made available for young people in these practices. I argue that relational, ideational, and material resources all support youths' development of identities—as it is through the taking up of these resources that they come to see themselves as particular kinds of people. It is through these resources that the possibilities for available identities are conveyed.

Controversies in Schooling as Identity-Building

Thus far, I have focused on the potentially positive aspects of the schools and programs that I have described in this chapter for supporting the racial and academic identities of African American students. However, the descriptions of these schools and programs also raise at least two important controversies with respect to educating African American students. The first highlights the potential tension between identity work and attention to academic content. Does the learning of important content—such as mathematics, writing, and history—suffer if teachers spend time supporting students' identities? The second controversy centers on whether this identity work requires learning contexts that are racially homogenous: in other words, does the learning setting have to be all African American for this identity work to happen? Moreover, what is to be said of all–African American learning environments?

Supporting Identity versus Teaching Content

A point of tension in this work is whether or not the work of supporting identities is just too "soft" and time-consuming in an educational system that is increasingly pressured to cover adequate amounts of material and prepare students to take high-stakes standardized tests. However, I think it is a mistake to view these two endeavors as mutually exclusive. First, identity-building work is directly related to engagement, and without the engagement of students not much learning (or test preparation for that matter) can occur. A second important aspect of identity-building work is the high academic expectations and rigorous standards to which students are held. In other words, strong academic preparation is a core part of supporting academic identities and thwarting racial stereotypes. This was quite evident for the segregated black schools in the South. For instance, in *Black Teachers on Teaching*, Foster (1997) notes that there was very little talk among the black teachers whom she interviewed about explicit identity-building. What stood out in their narratives was a consistent set of high expectations and the demand that students do high-quality work. In other words, rather than see academic excellence as being antithetical to supporting strong identities, it must be viewed as very much a part of the work of supporting identities. As students learn and see their own developing expertise in a discipline, their identities as strong students are also encouraged and their connection to limiting stereotypes about race is reduced.

All–African American Learning Environments?

Two of the three settings described in this chapter were all–African American settings; PMG was mostly African American. This raises the question, Is this a necessary characteristic of settings that support identity for African American students? In some ways, this is an empirical question that we can answer only with data. What is clear, however, is that the youth in these programs and schools felt that the African American adults in these learning settings were important to their experiences in these contexts and to their access to positive racialized and academic identities. Additionally, there was likely something important about the racially homogenous peer group, whereby the youth grappled with similar identity issues and stereotypes.

However, it is likely that discussions about identity and access to resources for academic identity could also occur in contexts that are not entirely African American. In 1935 W. E. B. Du Bois published an article called "Does the Negro Need All-Black Schools?" in which he argued that theoretically the answer to this question is a resounding "no." In a world where all teachers give all students equal opportunities to learn, assume that they are smart and capable, and are emotionally nurturing, there is no need for all-black schools. The problem, from Du Bois's perspective, was that the schools at that time were not such places. Black students endured routine and intense discrimination and oppression in white institutions, and under these conditions, Du Bois argued that for the time being, all-black schools were necessary.

This logic may still be appropriate as we consider this question today. The critical components of a learning environment that support the racialized and academic identities of students may not involve the race of the teachers or program leaders so much as their ability to deeply care for African American students, to believe in their potential to learn, and to understand the unique struggles they will face in a racialized world. While it is not the case that only African Americans can design and provide such a learning environment, it is more likely that they would have the experiences and perspectives to do so in especially meaningful ways.

Conclusions

This chapter has pointed to the critical nature of offering students school contexts where they are provided not only with rich learning opportunities, but also with opportunities to develop positive racialized and academic identities. I have drawn on several examples of schools and programs that integrate the support of African American students' racialized and academic identities into the work that they do with youth and have considered the types of material, ideational, and relational resources available to youth in these settings in support of racialized and academic identities.

These examples provide a set of ideas that can advance a conversation about how learning settings can be designed to support the racialized and academic identities of African American youth. What I have offered here should not be taken as prescription, but rather as inspiration—both for better theoretical accounts of these processes and better design work in schools and classrooms.

In 1933, when Carter G. Woodson wrote *The Mis-Education of the Negro*, he detailed several concerns about the dangers of not fully educating African Americans to be competitive in the world and espoused a need for them to understand their own history and to be dedicated to the "upliftment" of the African American race. Woodson worried about the production of an educated mass that could not serve the people or be a positive force in the community. Teaching for identity-building is essential to the goal of better supporting educational outcomes for African American youth and could help negate the kinds of fears Woodson expressed more than seventy years ago. Such identity work has potential for creating spaces where youth are not hamstrung by negative stereotypes about African Americans that are so prevalent in our society, and for encouraging positive change, not just in the lives of individual African American youth, but throughout African American communities and our nation.

Notes

1. Much of the discussion in this section is based on Vanessa Siddle-Walker's historical case study of Caswell County Training School, a segregated African American school in rural North Carolina.

2. I do not intend to suggest that all things at NCDC are good or that all people act the same way in this setting with respect to racial socialization practices.

Appendix
The Studies and Methodology

This book is the culmination of a decade of research by myself and colleagues on the learning experiences and identities of African American students. As such, I draw on data from several studies, and here I describe the studies upon which the chapters draw. They include four research studies on learning and identity in practices outside of school, including studies on middle and high school basketball (Nasir, 2000, 2002; Nasir and Hand, 2006), the game of dominoes (Nasir, 2002, 2005), and high school track and field (Nasir and Cooks, 2009), which provide the data for Chapter 2. They also include two studies on identity, learning, and achievement in school. One was a study of connection and disconnection and racial identity in an urban high school (Nasir, Jones, and McLaughlin, 2009; Nasir, McLaughlin, and Jones, in press), from which the data for Chapters 4 and 5 are drawn. The other is a study of racial identity, math identities, and math learning in a diverse high school (Nasir et al., 2009), which provides the data for Chapter 3. Here, I briefly describe the scope and focus of these studies and provide an overview of the research methods (more details of the methods for each study are available in the published articles cited above). I also present a basic description of the game of dominoes.

Studies on Learning in Cultural Practices Outside of School
High School Basketball

I conducted two studies that focused on different aspects of the practice of high school basketball. The first was concerned with understanding the nature of the mathematical thinking players engaged in as a part of the practice of basketball. This work also explored how this mathematical thinking (about player statistics and concepts of average and percent) was organized in relation to the structure of the practice of basketball as a whole. Methods included observations of middle and high school basketball players (sixteen middle school players and eighteen high school players) and interviews with the high school players and twelve high school students who were not players. The second study on basketball focused on the nature of learning in the sport more generally and compared the social organization of learning with the social organization of learning in the high school math classrooms of the players. This work also sought to understand the identities that players were constructing in these basketball and school mathematics practices. Methods included observation (video and field notes) of eight players across school math and basketball settings and interviews with them on math and basketball learning, achievement, and student identities.

Dominoes

The study on dominoes was a developmental study of domino play among African American elementary, high school, and adult players. Participants included twenty-nine elementary school players, thirty-two high school players, and thirteen adult players. This study was concerned with detailing thinking and learning in the game of dominoes, as well as how that learning was supported by the social organization of play. Players were given surveys about the history of their domino play, they were observed and videotaped during game play, and they were presented with standardized tasks so I could closely analyze the nature of their problem-solving in the context of the game.

Track and Field

This study focused on how teaching and learning happened for high school African American students and track coaches in the context of track and field. The sample included observations of a team of thirty athletes—their track practices and games—and informal and formal interviews with the athletes. Data also included weekly analysis sessions with the coach and audiotaped interactions between athletes and coaches during track meets and practices.

Studies on Learning and Identities in School
Connected and Disconnected Youth in an Urban High School

This study focused on the nature of connection and disconnection to school for African American high school students at a large, poorly performing public urban high school. Research explored pathways of connection and disconnection. These issues of connection were linked to issues of identity; that is, students who were more connected tended to have more highly developed academic identities. The everyday patterns of school connection and disconnection as well as the longer-term trajectories of students were studied using a range of methodological approaches, including interviews with seven focus students and eight teachers, administrators, and staff; extensive school and classroom observations and shadowing of seven focus students for eight school days each; long-term focus groups involving thirty students that met regularly; and a schoolwide survey of 121 students.

Racial Identities, Math Identities, and Learning in High School Math Classes

This study focused on documenting the ways that racial identities shaped learning and achievement in math classes at a large, diverse public high school. Our work included observations of students in math classes, interviews with African American students, and a survey. We conducted weekly observations in math classrooms, ranging from basic to more advanced classes. We also interviewed sixty-eight students regarding their perceptions of the school, experiences in math classrooms, and perceptions of who they are as racial group members and as math learners. Finally, we conducted a survey of more than five hundred students that explored students' racial, mathematical, and academic identities as well as issues of connection, disconnection, and achievement. Although the school was multiracial, our qualitative data focused largely on the experiences of African American students.

The Game of Dominoes

No one is quite sure when and where the game of dominoes originated or the source of its name. However, in the African American community, dominoes has been played for generations and has a rich history. Many players and nonplayers alike recognize it as more than a game, as an integral part of African American culture. Hence, in many African American communities, domino play is widespread. It is played at social gatherings, local parks and recreation centers, high school and college campuses, and senior citizen centers and involves players from small children to the elderly. There are many types of domino games, but here I focus on a version of the game in which participants make plays to score points. This is the version of play that I depict in the book.

Domino Rules

The materials used in domino play consist of twenty-eight tiles as depicted in the first illustration. Each tile is separated into two halves, and on each half is a number (represented by spots) from 0 (a blank half) to 6. The full set includes every possible combination of numbers from 0 to 6, including doubles. A game begins with four players each drawing seven dominoes from the set randomly arranged and placed facedown on a table.

The person who draws the double six (6–6) plays first. Players take turns and must match the end of a domino from their hand with an end square on the table. If the play results in a sum of all end dominoes as a multiple of five, then the player receives those points. If the sum is not a multiple of five, then no points are made.

For example, the second illustration shows the first four plays of a domino game. The player who drew the 6–6 begins and places it on the table. The next player follows with the 6–2, resulting in the total number of spots on the ends being 14 (6 + 6 + 2 = 14), which is not a multiple of five and hence no points are made. The third player plays the 6–3 on the 6–6, resulting in a total of 5 end spots (2 + 3 = 5), which is a score of five points. The fourth player follows up by playing the 3–3 on the 6–3, resulting in the total number of end spots being 8 (2 + 3 + 3 = 8), which is not a score.

Pairs of individuals play in teams against one another, and ideally players work to both block the opposing team from scoring and assist their partner in scoring. As players are engaged in the play of the game, they are faced with making many types of decisions, from choosing an opening play from all seven of their initial tiles, to making in-game decisions in the hopes of scoring points and winning games. The potential

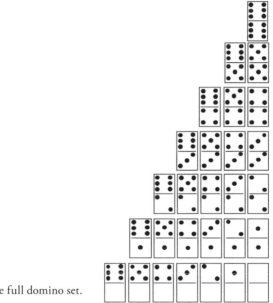

The full domino set.

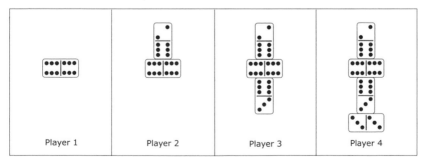

| Player 1 | Player 2 | Player 3 | Player 4 |

A sequence of domino plays.

complexity of game play and the wide range of skill with which players of different ages play this game afford a rich exploration of cultural and cognitive developmental processes in game play. Furthermore, help (in many forms) is integral to game play in that both during game play and in a postgame wrap-up, players often elaborate on the purposes of and thinking behind play choices, as well as offer commentary and assistance on the play of others.

References

Ainsworth-Darnell, J. W., and D. Downey. 1998. Assessing the oppositional culture explanation for racial/ethnic differences in school performance. *American Sociological Review*, 63(4), 536–553.

Akom, A. 2008. Black metropolis and mental life: Beyond the burden of acting white towards a third wave of critical racial studies. *Anthropology and Education Quarterly*, 39(3), 247–265.

American Anthropological Association. 1998. *American Anthropological Association statement on "race."* May 17. http://www.aaanet.org/stmts/racepp.htm.

Anderson, J. D. 1988. *The education of blacks in the South, 1860–1935*. Chapel Hill: University of North Carolina Press.

Ashmore, H. S. 1954. *The Negro and the schools*. Chapel Hill: University of North Carolina Press.

Bailey, A. 2006. Year in the life of an African American male in advertising: A content analysis. *Journal of Advertising*, 35(1), 83–104.

Balfanz, R., and N. Letgers. 2004. Locating the dropout crisis. Which high schools produce the nation's dropouts? Where are they located? Who attends them? Report 70, Center for Research on the Education of Students Placed at Risk, Johns Hopkins University.

Ball, A., and S. Brice-Heath. 1993. Dances of identity: Finding an ethnic self in the arts. In S. B. Heath and M. McLaughlin (eds.), *Identity and inner-city youth: Beyond ethnicity and gender*. New York: Teachers College. 69–93.

Baron, A., and M. Banaji. 2006. The development of implicit attitudes: Evidence of race evaluations from ages 6 and 10 and adulthood. *Psychological Science*, 17(1), 53–58.

Blackwell, A. G., S. Kwoh, and M. Pastor. 2002. *Searching for the uncommon common ground: New dimensions on race in America*. New York: Norton.

Boaler, J. 1999. Participation, knowledge, and beliefs: A community perspective on mathematics learning. *Educational Studies in Mathematics*, 40, 259–281.

Boaler, J., and J. G. Greeno. 2000. Identity, agency, and knowing in mathematics worlds. In J. Boaler (ed.), *Multiple perspectives on mathematics teaching and learning.* Westport, CT: Ablex. 171–200.

Bobo, L. 1999. Prejudice as social position: Microfoundations of a sociological approach to race and racism. *Journal of Social Issues,* 55(3), 445–472.

———. 2001. Racial attitude and relations at the close of the twentieth century. In N. Smelser, W. J. Wilson, and F. Mitchell (eds.), *America becoming: Racial trends and their consequences,* Vol. 1. Washington, DC: National Research Council. 264–301.

Bonilla-Silva, E. 2006. *Racism without racists: Color blind racism and the persistence of racial inequality in the United States.* New York: Rowman and Littlefield.

Bourdieu, P. 1977. *Outline of a theory of practice.* New York: Cambridge University Press.

Bowman, P., and C. Howard. 1985. Race-related socialization, motivation, and academic achievement: A study of black youths in three-generation families. *Journal of the American Academy of Child Psychiatry,* 24, 134–141.

Boykin, W., and F. D. Toms. 1985. Black child socialization: A conceptual framework. In H. P. McAdoo and J. L. McAdoo (eds.), *Black children: Social, educational, and parental environments.* Newbury Park, CA: Sage. 33–51.

Bransford, J., A. Brown, and R. Cocking (eds.). 2000. *How people learn: Brain, mind, experience, and school.* Washington, DC: National Academy Press.

Bronfenbrenner, U. 1979. *The ecology of human development: Experiments by nature and by design.* Cambridge, MA: Harvard University Press.

———. 1986. Ecology of the family as a context for human development: Research perspectives. *Developmental Psychology,* 22(6), 723–742.

———. 1993. The ecology of cognitive development. In R. H. Wozniak and K. W. Fischer (eds.), *Development in context: Acting and thinking in specific environments.* Hillsdale, NJ: Erlbaum. 3–44.

Bulwa, D., W. Buchanan, and M. Yi. 2009. Behind murder charge against ex-BART officer. *San Francisco Chronicle.* SFGate. January 15. http://www.sfgate.com/cgi-bin/article.cgi?f=/c/a/2009/01/15/MNJE15A6O2.DTL.

Burris, C., and K. Welner. 2005. Closing the achievement gap by detracking. *Phi Delta Kappan,* 86(8), 594–598.

Carter, D. 2008. Achievement as resistance: The development of a critical race achievement ideology among black achievers. *Harvard Educational Review,* 78(3), 466–497.

Carter, P. 2005. *Keeping it real.* New York: Oxford University Press.

Caughy, M. O., P. J. O'Campo, S. M. Randolph, and K. Nickerson. 2002. The influence of racial socialization practices on the cognitive and behavioral competence of African American preschoolers. *Child Development,* 73, 1611–1625.

Chan, D. 2005. Playing with race: The ethics of racialized representations in E-games. *International Review of Information Ethics,* 4, 25–29.

Clark, K., and M. Clark. 1939. The development of consciousness of self and the emergence of racial identification in Negro preschool children. *Journal of Social Psychology, SPSSI Bulletin*, 10, 591–599.

Cole, M. 1996. *Cultural psychology: A once and future discipline*. Cambridge, MA: Harvard University Press.

Conchas, G. 2001. Structuring failure and success: Understanding variability in Latino school engagement. *Harvard Educational Review*, 71(3), 475–504.

Constantine, M., and S. Blackmon. 2002. Black adolescents' racial socialization experiences: Their relations to home, school, and peer self-esteem. *Journal of Black Studies*, 32(3), 322–335.

Cooley, C. 1922. *Human nature and the social order*. New York: Scribner.

Crocker, J., and B. Major. 1989. Social stigma and self-esteem: The self-protective property of stigma. *Psychological Review*, 96(4), 608–630.

Cross, W. 1991. *Shades of black: Diversity in African American identity*. Philadelphia: Temple University Press.

Dance, L. J. 2002. *Tough fronts: The impact of street culture on schooling*. New York: Routledge.

Darling-Hammond, L. 2000. New standards and old inequalities: School reform and the education of African American students. *Journal of Negro Education*, 69(4), 263–287.

———. 2010. *The flat world and education: How America's commitment to equity will determine our future*. New York: Teachers College.

Darling-Hammond, L., J. A. Williamson, and M. Hyler. 2008. Securing the right to learn: The quest for empowering curriculum for African American citizens. *Journal of Negro Education*, 76(3), 281–296.

Davidson, A. 1996. *Making and molding identities in schools: Student narratives on race, gender, and academic engagement*. Albany: State University of New York.

Deburg, W. L. 2004. *Hoodlums: Black villains and social bandits in American life*. Chicago: University of Chicago Press.

Demo, D. H., and M. Hughes. 1990. Socialization and racial identity among black Americans. *Social Psychology Quarterly*, 53, 364–374.

Devine, P., and A. Elliott. 1995. Are racial stereotypes really fading? The Princeton trilogy revisited. *Personality and Social Psychology Bulletin*, 21(11), 1139–1150.

Douglass, Frederick. 1894. Blessings of liberty and education. September 3, Manassas, Virginia. TeachingAmericanHistory.org. http://teachingamericanhistory.org/library/index.asp?document=543.

Drake, S. 1987. *Black folk here and there*. Los Angeles: Center for Afro-American Studies.

Du Bois, W. E. B. 1903. *The souls of black folk*. Chicago: McClurg.

———. 1935. Does the Negro need separate schools? *Journal of Negro Education*, 4, 328–335.

Eccles, J. S., and J. A. Gootman. 2002. *Community programs to promote youth development*.

Committee on Community-Level Programs for Youth. Board on Children, Youth, and Families, Commission on Behavioral and Social Sciences and Education, National Research Council and Institute of Medicine. Washington, DC: National Academy Press.

Engestrom, Y. 1999. Activity theory and individual and social transformation. In Y. Engestrom, R. Miettinen, and R. Punamaki (eds.), *Perspectives on activity theory*. New York: Cambridge University Press. 19–38.

Erikson, E. 1959. Identity and the life cycle: Selected papers. *Psychological Issues*, 1, 1–171.

———. 1968. *Identity: Youth and crisis*. New York: Norton.

Essed, P. 2002. Everyday racism: A new approach to the study of racism. In P. Essed and D. Goldenberg (eds.). *Race critical theories: Test and context*. Malden, MA: Blackwell. 176–194.

Ferguson, A. 2000. *Bad boys: Public schools in the making of black masculinity*. Ann Arbor: University of Michigan Press.

Ferguson, R. 2007. *Toward excellence with equity: An emerging vision for closing the achievement gap*. Cambridge, MA: Harvard University Press.

Fordham, S. 1991. Racelessness in private schools. *Teacher College Record*, 92(3), 470–484.

———. 1996. *Blacked out: Dilemmas of race, identity, and success at Capital High*. Chicago: University of Chicago Press.

Fordham, S., and J. Ogbu. 1986. Black students' school success: Coping with the burden of "acting white." *Urban Review*, 18, 176–206.

Foster, M. 1997. *Black teachers on teaching*. New York: Norton.

Frederickson, G. 2002. *Racism: A short history*. Princeton, NJ: Princeton University Press.

Gallimore, R., C. Goldenberg, and T. Weisner. 1993. The social construction and subjective reality of activity settings: Implications for community psychology. *American Journal of Community Psychology*, 21(4), 537–560.

Gamoran, A. 1987. The stratification of high school learning opportunities. *Sociology of Education*, 60, 135–155.

———. 1992. The variable effects of high school tracking. *American Sociological Review*, 57(6), 812–828.

Gay, G. 2000. *Culturally responsive teaching: Theory, research, practice*. New York: Teachers College.

Goffman, E. 1959. *The presentation of self in everyday life*. New York: Doubleday.

———. 1963. *Stigma: Notes on the management of spoiled identity*. New York: Simon and Schuster.

———. 1974. *Frame analysis: An essay on the organization of experience*. Cambridge, MA: Harvard University Press.

Gonzalez, N., L. C. Moll, and C. Amanti. 2005. *Funds of knowledge: Theorizing practices in households, communities, and classrooms*. New York: Routledge.

Goodman, B., and R. Dretzin (producers). 2001. *Merchants of cool*. Frontline PBS Special. Aired on February 27, 2001.

Graham, S., A. Taylor, and C. Hudley. 1998. Exploring achievement values among ethnic minority early adolescents. *Journal of Educational Psychology*, 91, 606–620.

Greeno, J. 2006. Learning in activity. In K. Sawyer (ed.), *The Cambridge handbook of the learning sciences*. New York: Cambridge University Press.

Grubb, N., and M. Lazerson. 2004. *The education gospel: The economic power of schooling*. Cambridge, MA: Harvard University Press.

Gutiérrez, K. 2004. *Rethinking education policy for English learners*. Washington, DC: Aspen Institute.

Gutiérrez, K., and B. Rogoff. 2003. Cultural ways of learning: Individual traits of cultural repertoires of practice. *Educational Researcher*, 32(5), 19–25.

Gutierrez, R. 2008. A "gap-gazing" fetish in mathematics education? Problematizing research on the achievement gap. *Journal of Research in Mathematics Education*, 39(4), 357–364.

Haycock, K. 1998. Good teaching matters: How well-qualified teachers can close the gap. Unpublished report. Washington, DC: Education Trust.

Haycock, K., C. Jerald, and S. Huang. 2001. Closing the gap: Done in a decade. *Thinking K–16*, 5(2), 3–21.

Heath, S. B. 2004. Risks, rules, and roles: Youth perspectives on the work of learning for community development. In A. N. Perret-Clemont, C. Pontecorvo, L. B. Resnick, T. Zittoun, and B. Burge (eds.), *Joining society: Social interaction and learning in adolescence and youth*. New York: Cambridge University Press. 41–70.

Heath, S. B., and M. McLaughlin (eds.). 1993. *Identity and inner-city youth: Beyond ethnicity and gender*. New York: Teachers College.

Helms, J. 1990. *Black and white racial identity: Theory, research, and practice*. Westport, CT: Praeger.

Herrenkohl, L., and J. Wertsch. 1999. The use of cultural tools: Mastery and appropriation. In I. Sigel (ed.), *Development of mental representation*. Mahwah, NJ: Erlbaum. 415–436.

Hirsch, B. 2005. *A place to call home: After-school programs for urban youth*. New York: Teachers College.

Holland, D., W. Lachicotte, D. Skinner, and C. Cain. 1998. *Identity and agency in cultural worlds*. Cambridge, MA: Harvard University Press.

Hudley, C., and S. Graham. 2001. Stereotypes of achievement striving among early adolescents. *Social Psychology of Education*, 5, 201–224.

Hughes, D., and L. Chen. 1997. When and what parents tell children about race: An examination of race-related socialization among African American families. *Applied Developmental Science*, 1(4), 200–214.

Hughes, D., and D. Johnson. 2001. Correlates in children's expectations of parents' racial socialization behaviors. *Journal of Marriage and the Family*, 63(4), 981–995.

Hughes, D., E. Smith, H. Stevenson, J. Rodriguez, D. Johnson, and P. Spicer. 2006.

Parents' ethnic-racial socialization practices: A review of research and directions for future study. *Developmental Psychology*, 42(5), 747–770.

Jhally, S. 1997. *bell hooks: Cultural criticism and transformation*. DVD.

Johnson, D. J. 1994. Parental racial socialization among middle class black children. In J. McAdoo (ed.), *XIII Empirical Conference in Black Psychology*. East Lansing: Michigan State University. 17–38.

Keating, A. 1995. Interrogating "whiteness," (de)constructing "race." *College English*, 57(8), 901–918.

Kim, D. 2004. Youth development in a community technology center: Negotiation of "off-the-record-learning" with technology. PhD diss., Stanford University.

Kluger, R. 1975. *Simple justice*. New York: Random House.

Kozol, J. 2005. *The shame of the nation: The restoration of apartheid schooling in America*. New York: Crown.

Krueger, J. 1996. Personal beliefs and cultural stereotypes about racial characteristics. *Journal of Personality and Social Psychology*, 71, 536–548.

Ladson-Billings, G. 1995. *The dreamkeepers*. San Francisco: Jossey-Bass.

———. 2006. From the achievement gap to the education debt: Understanding achievement in U.S. schools. *Educational Researcher*, 35(7), 3–12.

Lankford, H., S. Loeb, and J. Wyckoff. 2002. Teacher sorting and the plight of urban schools: A descriptive analysis. *Educational Evaluation and Policy Analysis*, 24(1), 37–62.

Larson, R. W., M. H. Richards, B. Sims, and J. Dworkin. 2001. How urban African-American adolescents spend their time: Time budgets for locations, activities, and companionship. *American Journal of Community Psychology*, 29(4), 565–597.

Larson, R. W., and S. Verma. 1999. How children and adolescents spend time across the world: Work, play, and developmental opportunities. *Psychological Bulletin*, 125, 701–736.

Lave, J., and E. Wenger. 1991. *Situated learning and legitimate peripheral participation*. Cambridge: Cambridge University Press.

Lee, C. 2008. The centrality of culture to the scientific study of learning and development: How an ecological framework in education research facilitates civic responsibility. *Educational Researcher*, 37, 267–279.

———. 2009. Profile of an independent black institution: African-centered education at work. In C. Payne and C. Strickland (eds.), *Teach freedom: Education for liberation in the African American tradition*. New York: Teachers College. 208–222.

Lee, C. D. 1995. Signifying as a scaffold for literary interpretation. *Journal of Black Psychology*, 21(4), 357–381.

———. 2007. *Culture, literacy, and learning: Blooming in the midst of a whirlwind*. New York: Teachers College.

Lee, C. D., and Y. Majors. 2003. "Heading up the street": Localized opportunities for shared constructions of knowledge. *Pedagogy, Culture and Society*, 11(1), 49–67.

Leontiev, A. 1978. The problem of activity in psychology. In J. V. Werstch (ed.), *The concept of activity in Soviet psychology*. New York: Sharpe. 37–71.

Lerner, R. 1991. Changing organism-context relations as the basic process of development: A developmental contextual perspective. *Developmental Psychology*, 27(1), 27–32.

Levinson, B., D. Foley, and D. Holland. 1996. *The cultural production of the educated person: Critical ethnographies of schooling and local practice*. Albany: State University of New York.

Lewin, K. 1935. *A dynamic theory of personality*. London: McGraw-Hill.

———. 1951. *Field theory in social science*. New York: Harper Brothers.

Lewis, A. 2003. Race in the schoolyard: Negotiating the color line in classrooms and communities. New Brunswick, NJ: Rutgers University Press.

Majors, Y. 2003. Shoptalk: Teaching and learning in an African American hair salon. *Mind, Culture and Activity*, 10(4), 289–310.

Marica, J. E. 1966. Development and validation of ego-identity status. *Journal of Personality and Social Psychology*, 3(5), 551–558.

———. 1980. Identity in adolescence. In J. Adelson (ed.), *Handbook of adolescent psychology*. New York: Wiley. 159–187.

Markus, H., and Z. Kunda. 1986. Stability and malleability of the self-concept. *Journal of Personality and Social Psychology*, 51(4), 858–866.

Marshall, S. 1995. Ethnic socialization of African American children: Implications for parenting, identity development, and academic achievement. *Journal of Youth and Adolescence*, 24, 377–396.

Martin, D. B. 2009. Liberating the production of knowledge about African American children and mathematics. In D. Martin (ed.), *Mathematics teaching, learning, and liberation in African-American contexts*. New York: Routledge. 3–38.

Massey, D. 2007. *Categorically unequal: The American stratification system*. New York: Russell Sage Foundation.

McDermott, R., and H. Varenne. 1995. Culture as disability. *Anthropology and Education Quarterly*, 26(3), 324–348.

McKown, C., and R. Weinstein. 2003. The development and consequences of stereotype consciousness in middle childhood. *Child Development*, 74(2), 498–515.

Mead, G. H. 1934. *Mind, self, and society*. Chicago: University of Chicago Press.

Mehan, H. 1996. *Constructing school success: The consequences of placing low achieving students in high track classes*. Cambridge: Cambridge University Press.

Mehan, H., L. Hubbard, and I. Villanueva. 1994. Forming academic identities: Accommodation without assimilation among involuntary minorities. *Anthropology and Education Quarterly*, 25(2), 91–117.

Mikelson, R., and A. Velasco. 2006. Bring it on! Diverse responses to "acting white" among academically able black adolescents. In E. Horvat and C. O'Connor (eds.), *Beyond acting white*. New York: Rowman and Littlefield. 27–65.

Miller, D. 1999. Racial socialization and racial identity: Can they promote resiliency for African American adolescents? *Adolescence*, 34(135), 493–501.

Moll, L., and N. González. 2004. Engaging life: A funds of knowledge approach to multicultural education. In J. Banks and C. McGee Banks (eds.), *Handbook of research on multicultural education*. 2nd ed. New York: Jossey-Bass. 699–715.

Moody, V. 2004. Sociocultural orientations and the mathematical success of African American students. *Journal of Educational Research*, 97(3), 135–146.

Morgan, S., and J. Mehta. 2004. Beyond the laboratory: Evaluating the survey evidence for the disidentification explanation of black-white differences in achievement. *Sociology of Education*, 77(1), 82–101.

Morris, J. E. 2001. Forgotten voices of African-American educators: Critical race perspectives on the implementation of a desegregation plan. *Educational Policy*, 15(4), 575–600.

Morris, R. 2008. "We are rising as a people": The content of instruction in Freedman's School. In C. Payne and C. S. Strickland (eds.), *Teach Freedom: Education for Liberation in the African American Tradition*. New York: Teachers College. 19–24.

Nasir, N. 2000. "Points ain't everything": Emergent goals and average and percent understandings in the play of basketball among African-American students. *Anthropology and Education Quarterly*, 31(3), 283–305.

———. 2002. Identity, goals, and learning: Mathematics in cultural practice. *Mathematical thinking and learning*, 4(2/3), 213–248.

———. 2004. "Halal-ing" the child: Reframing identities of opposition in an urban Muslim school. *Harvard Educational Review*, 74(2), 153–174.

———. 2005. Individual cognitive structuring and the sociocultural context: Strategy shifts in the game of dominoes. *Journal of the Learning Sciences*, 14(1), 5–34.

———. 2008. Everyday pedagogy: Lessons from track, basketball, and dominoes. *Phi Delta Kappan Magazine*, 89(7), 529–532.

———. 2010. Studying identity in learning contexts from a human sciences perspective. *Learning Research as a Human Science*, 109(1), 53–65.

Nasir, N., and J. Cooks. 2009. Becoming a hurdler: How learning settings afford identities. *Anthropology and Education Quarterly*, 40(1), 41–61.

Nasir, N., M. Davis, G. Atukpawu, and K. O'Connor. 2009. Wrestling with stereotypes: Being African American in math class. In D. Martin (ed.), *Mathematics teaching, learning, and liberation in African-American contexts*. New York: Routledge. 231–248.

Nasir, N., and V. Hand. 2006. Exploring socio-cultural perspectives on race, culture, and learning. *Review of Educational Research*, 76(4), 449–476.

———. 2008. From the court to the classroom: Opportunities for engagement, learning, and identity in basketball and classroom mathematics. *Journal of the Learning Sciences*, 17(2), 143–161.

Nasir, N., A. Jones, and M. McLaughlin. 2009. What does it mean to be African American? Constructions of racial/ethnic identity and school performance in an urban public high school. *American Educational Research Journal*, 46(1), 73–114.

Nasir, N., M. McLaughlin, and A. Jones. In press. School connectedness for students in low-income urban high schools. *Teachers College Record*.

Nasir, N., and G. Saxe. 2003. Ethnic and academic identities: A cultural practice perspective on emerging tensions and their management in the lives of minority students. *Educational Researcher*, 32(5), 14–18.

Nasir, N. S., B. Warren, A. Roseberry, and C. Lee. 2006. Learning as a cultural process: Achieving equity through diversity. In K. Sawyer (ed.), *Cambridge handbook of the learning sciences*. New York: Cambridge University Press. 489–504.

National Center for Education Statistics. 2005. *The condition of education 2005*. Washington, DC: U.S. Department of Education.

———. 2007. *Dropout rates in the US: 2005*. Washington, DC: U.S. Department of Education.

Newby, R., and D. Tyack. 1971. Victims without "crimes": Some historical perspectives on black education. *Journal of Negro Education*, 40(3), 192–206.

Noddings, N. 1992. *The challenge to care in schools*. New York: Teachers College.

Oakes, J. 2004. Inequality, stratification, and the struggle for just schooling. Lecture delivered at the annual meeting of the International Conference of the Learning Sciences, Los Angeles, June.

O'Connor, C. 1997. Dispositions toward (collective) struggle and educational resilience in the inner city: A case study of six African American high school students. *American Educational Research Journal*, 34(4), 593–629.

———. 1999. Race, class, and gender in America: Narratives of opportunity among low-income African American youths. *Sociology of Education*, 72 (July), 137–157.

O'Connor, C., E. Horvat, and A. Lewis. 2006. Framing the field: Past and future research on the historic underachievement of black students. In E. Horvat and C. O'Connor (eds.), *Beyond acting white*. New York: Rowman and Littlefield. 1–24.

O'Connor, K., and W. Penuel. 2010. Introduction: Principles of a human sciences approach to research on learning. *Learning Research as a Human Science*, 109(1), 1–16.

O'Connor, L.A., J. Brooks-Gunn, and J. Graber. 2000. Black and white girls' racial preference in media and peer choices and the role of socialization for black girls. *Journal of Family Psychology*, 14, 510–521.

Ogbu, J. 1987. Variability in minority school performance: A problem in search of an explanation. *Anthropology and Education Quarterly*, 18(4), 312–334.

———. 1992. Adaptation to minority status and impact on school success. *Theory into Practice*, 31, 287–295.

Omi, M., and H. Winant. 1994. *Racial formation in the United States: From the 1960s to the 1990s*. New York: Routledge.

Orfield, G. 2001. Schools more separate: Consequences of a decade of resegregation. Report of the Civil Rights Project. Harvard University.

Osbourne, J. 1997. Race and academic disidentification. *Journal of Educational Psychology*, 89, 728–735.

Oyserman, D., K. Harrison, and D. Bybee. 2001. Can racial identity be predictive of academic efficacy? *The International Journal for the Study of Behavioural Development*, 25(4), 379–385.

Oyserman, D., S. Kemmelmeier, H. Fryber, T. Brosh, and T. Hart-Johnson. 2003. Racial-ethnic self-schemas. *Social Psychology Quarterly*, 66(4), 333–347.

Page, H. 1997. "Black male" imagery and media containment of African American men. *American Anthropologist*, 99(1), 99–111.

Perry, T. 2003. Up from the parched earth: Toward a theory of African-American achievement. In T. Perry, C. Steele, and A. Hilliard (eds.), *Young, gifted and black: Promoting high achievement among African-American students*. Boston: Beacon Press. 1–108.

Pollock, M. 2005. *Colormute: Race talk dilemmas in an American school*. Princeton, NJ: Princeton University Press.

Ro, R. 1996. *Gangsta: Merchandizing the rhymes of violence*. New York: St. Martins.

Rogoff, B. 1993. *Apprenticeship in thinking*. New York: Oxford University Press.

———. 2003. *The cultural nature of human development*. New York: Oxford University Press.

Rome, D. 2004. *Black demons: The media's depiction of the African American male criminal stereotype*. Westport, CT: Greenwood.

Rose, M. 2004. *The mind at work*. New York: Viking.

Rumbaut, R. 1994. The crucible within: Ethnic identity, self-esteem, and segmented assimilation among children of immigrants. *International Migration Review*, xxviii(4), 748–794.

Sanders, M. G. 1997. Overcoming obstacles: Academic achievement as a response to racism and discrimination. *Journal of Negro Education*, 66(1), 83–93.

Sawyer, K. 2006. Introduction: The new science of learning. In K. Sawyer (ed.), *The Cambridge handbook of the learning sciences*. New York: Cambridge University Press.

Saxe, G. 1999. Cognition, development, and cultural practices. In E. Turiel (ed.), *Culture and development: New directions in child psychology*. San Francisco: Jossey-Bass. 19–35.

Schott Foundation. 2010. *Yes we can: The 2010 Schott report on black males in public education*. Cambridge, MA: Schott Foundation.

Scott, L. D. 2003. The relation of racial identity and racial socialization to coping with discrimination among African Americans. *Journal of Black Studies*, 33, 520–538.

Sellers, R., T. Chavous, and D. Cooke. 1998. Racial ideology and racial centrality as predictors of African American college students' academic performance. *Journal of Black Psychology*, 24, 8–27.

Shelton, J., and R. Sellers. 2000. Situational stability and variability in African American racial identity. *Journal of Black Psychology*, 26, 27–50.

Siddle-Walker, V. 1996. *Their highest potential: An African American school community in the segregated South*. Chapel Hill: University of North Carolina Press.

———. 2000. Valued segregated schools for African American children in the South, 1935–1969: A review of common themes and characteristics. *Review of Educational Research*, 70(13), 253–285.

Skinner, D., and R. Schafer. 2009. Performing race in four culturally diverse fourth grade classrooms: Silence, race talk, and the negotiation of social boundaries. *Anthropology and Education Quarterly*, 40(3), 277–296.

Sowell, T. 1974. Black excellence: The case of Dunbar High School. *Public Interest*, 35, 3–21.

Spencer, M. 1999. Social and cultural influences on school adjustment: The application of an identity-focused cultural ecological perspective. *Educational Psychologist*, 34(1), 43–57.

Spencer, M., E. Noll, J. Stolfus, and V. Harpalani. 2001. Identity and school adjustment: Revisiting the "acting white" assumption. *Educational Psychologist*, 36, 21–30.

Spencer, M. B. 1987. Black children's ethnic identity formation: Risk and resilience in castelike minorities. In J. Phinney and M. Rotheram (eds.), *Children's ethnic socialization: Pluralism and development*. Newbury Park, CA: Sage. 103–116.

———. 2006. Phenomenology and ecological systems theory: Development of diverse groups. In W. Damon and R. Lerner (eds.), *Handbook of child psychology, Vol. 1: Theoretical models of human development*. 6th ed. New York: Wiley. 829–893

———. 2008. Fourth Annual *Brown* Lecture in Education Research—Lessons learned and opportunities ignored since *Brown v. Board of Education*: Youth development and the myth of a color-blind society. *Educational Researcher*, 37, 253–266.

Stangor, C., and M. Schaller. 1996. Stereotypes as individual and collective representations. In C. Macrae, C. Stangor, and M. Hewstone (eds.), *Stereotypes and stereotyping*. New York: Guilford. 3–29.

Steele, C. 1997. A threat in the air: How stereotypes shape intellectual identity and performance. *American Psychologist*, 52, 613–629.

———. 1998. Stereotyping and its threats are real. *American Psychologist*, 53(6), 680–681.

Steele, C., and J. Aronson. 1995. Stereotype threat and the intellectual test performance of African Americans. *Journal of Personality and Social Psychology*, 69(5), 797–811.

Steele, S. 2008. Obama's post-racial promise. *Los Angeles Times*, November 5.

Stevens, R., and R. Hall. 1998. Disciplined perception: Learning to see in technoscience. In M. Lampert and M. L. Blunk (eds.), *Talking mathematics in school: Studies of teaching and learning*. Cambridge: Cambridge University Press. 107–149.

Stinson, D. 2008. Negotiating sociocultural discourses: The counter-storytelling of academically (and mathematically) successful African American male students. *American Educational Research Journal*, 45(4), 975–1010.

Stryker, S. 1987. Identity theory: Developments and extensions. In K. Yardley and T. Honess (eds.), *Self and identity: Psychosocial perspectives*. New York: Wiley. 89–105.

Stryker, S., and R. T. Serpe. 1994. Identity salience and psychological centrality: Equivalent, overlapping, or complementary concepts. *Social Psychology Quarterly*, 57(1), 16–35.

Tatum, B. 1992. African-American identity development, academic achievement, and missing history. *Social Education*, 56(6), 331–334.

———. 1997. *Why are all the black kids sitting together in the cafeteria?* New York: Basic Books.

Thornton, M. C., L. M. Chatters, R. J. Taylor, and W. R. Allen. 1990. Sociodemographic and environmental correlates of racial socialization by black parents. *Child Development*, 61, 401–409.

Tyson, K., W. Daroty, and D. Castellino. 2005. It's not "a black thing": Understanding the burden of acting white and other dilemmas of high achievement. *American Sociological Review*, 70(4), 582–605.

U.S. Census Bureau. 2008. School enrollment—Social and economic characteristics of students: October 2007. http://www.census.gov/population/www/socdemo/school/cps2007.html.

Van Ausdale, D., and J. R. Feagin. 2001. *The first R: How children learn race and racism*. New York: Rowman and Littlefield.

Varenne, H., and R. McDermott. 1998. *Successful failure: The school America builds*. Boulder, CO: Westview.

Viadero, D., and R. Johnson. 2001. Lags in minority achievement defy traditional explanations. *Education Week*, 19(28), 1–18.

Vygotsky, L. 1962. *Thought and language*. New York: Wiley.

———. 1978. *Mind in society: The development of higher psychological processes*. Cambridge, MA: Harvard University Press.

Watkins, W. 2001. *The white architects of black education: Ideology and power in America, 1865–1954*. New York: Teachers College.

Wenger, E. 1998. *Communities of practice: Learning, meaning, and identity*. Cambridge: Cambridge University Press.

Woodland, M., J. Martin, L. Hill, and F. Worrell. 2009. The most blessed room in the city: The influence of a youth development program on three young black males. *Journal of Negro Education*, 78(3), 233–245.

Woodson, C. G. 1933. The mis-education of the Negro. Washington, DC: Associated Publishers.

Wortham, S. 2006. *Learning identity: The joint emergence of social identification and academic learning.* New York: Cambridge University Press.

Yosso, T. 2005. Whose culture has capital? A critical race theory discussion of cultural wealth. *Race Ethnicity and Education*, 8(1), 69–91.

Index